TWAYNE'S WORLD LEADERS SERIES

EDITORS OF THIS VOLUME

Arthur W. Brown

Baruch College, The City University

of New York

and

Thomas S. Knight

Adelphi University

Puritanism in America
1620 - 1750

TWLS 71

John Winthrop   Cotton Mather

Increase Mather   John Cotton

PURITANISM IN AMERICA
1620 - 1750

By EVERETT EMERSON
University of Massachusetts

TWAYNE PUBLISHERS
A DIVISION OF G. K. HALL & CO., BOSTON

Library of Congress Cataloging in Publication Data

Emerson, Everett H   1925 -
    Puritanism in America, 1620 - 1750.

    (Twayne's world leaders series ; TWLS 71)
    Bibliography: p. 173 - 76
    Includes index.
    1.   Puritans—United States.   I.   Title.
BX9354.2.E47   285'.9'0973   77-4354
ISBN 0-8057-7692-3

MANUFACTURED IN THE UNITED STATES OF AMERICA

FOR
VIRGINIA AND THOMAS DAVIS

Contents

About the Author

Everett Emerson is professor of English at the University of Massachusetts, Amherst. Besides teaching duties in California, Florida, Pennsylvania, North Carolina, New York, and Virginia, he has undertaken the writing of a number of books: *John Cotton, Captain John Smith,* and *English Puritanism from John Hooper to John Milton.* In addition, he has edited *Major Writers of Early American Literature; Letters from New England, 1629 - 1638: The Massachusetts Bay Colony;* and *American Literature, 1764 - 1789: The Revolutionary Years.* He serves as a field editor for G. K. Hall and Company, and as general editor of the journal *Early American Literature.*

Preface

Earlier volumes in this series explore the Enlightenment and Transcendentalism in America. Before both of these important movements and significantly influencing each was Puritanism, an intellectual, cultural, and religious force whose power was most fully felt in New England. Puritanism has been explored again and again, and we are now in a position to understand it more fully than before. Unfortunately, the complexity of the subject has usually resulted in explorations so dense, so subtle, and so difficult as to be useful only to dedicated readers. The following study, while it does not pretend to be exhaustive, is also not, I hope, exhausting. It offers and overview of the historical development of Puritanism in the seventeenth and early eighteenth centuries, with particular attention to its ideas, the changes that took place within it, and its cultural contributions.

For help of various kinds I am indebted, first of all, to my wife Katherine and to my friends Thomas Davis and Mason Lowance. But I also thank, heartily, my colleague Cynthia Wolff, my friends Alberta Booth and David Drinkwater, and the staff of the Folger Library, where I began this study as a senior fellow.

I also acknowledge, with thanks, the courtesy of the American Antiquarian Society for permission to reproduce the portraits of Cotton Mather and John Winthrop, the Connecticut Historical Society for the portrait of John Cotton, and the Massachusetts Historical Society for the portrait of Increase Mather. The quotations from *The Poems of Edward Taylor*, edited by Donald Stanford (Yale University Press, 1960), are made by permission of the Yale University Press.

EVERETT EMERSON

Santa Barbara, California
February 16, 1977

Acknowledgments

The author thanks the organizations who made available the photographs appearing on the frontispiece:

John Winthrop and Cotton Mather: The American Antiquarian Society

Increase Mather and John Cotton: The Connecticut Historical Society

Introduction

Like it or not, Americans have a Puritan heritage, and to cope with it requires an understanding of it. The accident, if that is the word, behind this heritage, deserves attention, too. The events of man's history have been frequently shaped by accident. For a variety of reasons the seventeenth century was the time when what is now the eastern fringe of the United States was to be colonized, or, as Francis Jennings has persuasively put it, conquered; its original inhabitants overcome. It might have been the French or the Spanish who established the colonies that grew till they declared their independence a century and a half later. But it was Englishmen. In the colonies that grew most rapidly during the early years, the most powerful leaders were Puritans. Only briefly was there a time when English Puritans would want to migrate in numbers; only briefly was Puritanism a force powerful enough to attract leaders who would direct the difficult journey across the seas to an uncertain fate. The fact that New England was settled by these men and their followers has been largely responsible for the strange mixture of idealism and pragmatism that has been of such importance in the making of America. The outlook of the Puritans was particularly suited to the development of capitalism and democracy. When one has identified Puritanism with these terms—and there was much more to Puritanism—one has gone a long way towards describing the American character.

Paradoxically, the Puritan impulse bore two entirely different kinds of fruit. In England, the radical energies released by Puritanism eventually resulted in civil war, the overthrow of the royal government, and social disorder. In New England, these same energies were channeled into the creation of a commonwealth based on the conviction that discipline, law, and order were fundamental. A powerful unity, an organic relationship of state, church, and society, was created in New England. It flourished only briefly, but its effects were long felt.

In this study of American Puritanism—or, more accurately, of Puritanism in New England—I have attempted to trace the growth, development, and decline of Puritanism from its origins in sixteenth-century England. In the New World, Puritanism was interwoven with politics, social organization, church polity, economics, literature, child-rearing, in addition to specifically religious thought, and the pages that follow at least touch on all of these matters. The organization of the book is chiefly chronological and, after a preliminary exploration of the English background, covers the period from 1620, when the first Puritans came to New England, through about 1750, when the Great Awakening divided and disorganized much of what was left of the Puritan fabric in New England. Within this chronological frame I have placed two chapters that are less concerned with development and change: one concerning Puritan achievements—the pulpit eloquence of Thomas Hooker, the creation of Harvard College, and the poetry of Anne Bradstreet and Edward Taylor; and one that examines Puritan diaries to see how the introspective operations of four men's minds took place—Thomas Shepard, Michael Wigglesworth, Samuel Sewall, and Cotton Mather.

Puritanism did not disappear in the middle of the eighteenth century. The ideas and attitudes identified with it continued to be powerfully influential. I have not attempted here to provide a full report on the complicated issue of the Puritan heritage, for that is a subject deserving of separate study. But I have attempted to analyze those ideas and concerns that are the gift—or the burden—that the Puritans gave to Americans to come, such matters as how Puritanism encouraged introspection; how it emphasized man's utterly sinful nature; how it encouraged individualism; how it encouraged Americans to think of their nation as having a special mission in human history. Much of this study is devoted to theological considerations, but not pure theology: rather, the relationship of religious ideas to the human situation in early New England.

Because my task is a substantial one, I have inevitably chosen not to deal with many topics that other students of Puritanism may feel are as important as those I have selected. I have not, for example, taken up the fascinating topic of Salem witchcraft, for to understand it, one must consider factors apart from Puritanism. I have, however, tried to take advantage of many recent studies that shed light on Puritanism from a perspective rather remote from the strictly intellectual concerns of the great scholar of Puritanism, Perry Miller, notably the work of historians of such New England towns as Salem, Boston, Andover, and Dedham. These have contributed much to our knowledge of the life of the people of Puritan New England. But many brilliant minds have been employed in the study of Puritanism, and to provide a full synthesis of their findings is beyond the scope of this book. The pages that follow contain many quotations from the Puritans, for I think that there is value to hearing the tones, the attitudes, of writers and preachers, not just a summary of their ideas. To make these writings somewhat less remote, I have modernized spelling, capitalization, and punctuation.

What is American Puritanism? There is no easy answer, for it was constantly changing its shape, though it developed a strong sense of tradition, of devotion to the English fathers of Puritanism and to the founders of New England. Calvinism was a part of it, though its emphases were rather different from those of both John Calvin himself and the Continental theologians who came after him: Puritanism gave higher priority to preaching and to the process of salvation, and it was less concerned with strictly theological issues. It was developed in a new land, where Puritans could exercise substantial control of the life of the inhabitants and could keep those who were unsympathetic away, at least for a time. It was paradoxical. It emphasized church fellowship and taught that God worked through the relationship called the communion of the saints. But it demanded that man probe, privately but profoundly, his own soul, both to detect signs of faith and to root out hidden sins. It was highly intellectual and put a premium on education, but it also taught that what really motivates man is the heart, the affections. Puritanism was an activist, this-worldly kind of religion that denied the ultimate value of anything material. It was profoundly pessimistic about the nature of man but it encouraged a forward-looking attitude towards America.

There is much that is appealing about the Puritans and much that is appalling. The processes of change within Puritanism were both strange and natural—for instance, the fact that the radical Puritan fathers bred conservatives. Perhaps as we look at Puritanism we can learn something about human nature, about man as he was and as he is.

Chronology

1536   Henry VIII and the English Parliament separate the Church of England from Rome.

1547   Accession of Edward VI.

1549-   Disputes between conservatives and proto-Puritans about
1553   church ceremonial.

1553   Accession of Catholic Queen Mary. Some English Protestants flee to Continent.

1558   Elizabeth I accedes to the throne. Disputes begin within the Church of England, again independent of Rome, between conservatives and Puritans, the result being the Elizabethan Compromise, unsatisfactory to Puritans.

1572-   Debate between John Whitgift and Thomas Cartwright
1577   over the nature of the church.

1584-   William Perkins teaches and preaches at Cambridge Uni-
1602   versity.

1603   Accession of James I. Puritan hopes for reform are high but soon disappointed.

1606   Establishment of a Separatist congregation at Scrooby by group including William Bradford.

1615   John Cotton becomes a nonconformist.

1620   Separatists begin "Pilgrim" colony at Plymouth.

1623   Publication of William Ames's *Medulla Sacrae Theologiae*.

1625   Accession of Charles I, unsympathetic with Puritanism.

1628   William Laud becomes Bishop of London and begins anti-Puritan campaign.

1629   Massachusetts Bay Company charter granted.

1630   John Winthrop leads first large body of Puritans to Massachusetts Bay.

1634   Puritan movement to Connecticut begins.

1636   Founding of Harvard College.

1637   Roger Williams banished by Massachusetts Bay. Antinomian crisis. Synod of church leaders condemns Anne Hutchinson and her followers.

1640   Calling of Long Parliament. Migration to New England largely stops.

1646   Episcopacy abolished in the Church of England.

1649   Publication of Cambridge Platform.

1651   Publication of Anne Bradstreet's poems, *The Tenth Muse.*

1660   Accession of Charles II. Episcopal polity re-established in Church of England.

1660-   Jeremiads preached by many Puritan ministers.
1690

1661   Synod adopts "Half-Way Covenant."

1671   Edward Taylor moves to Westfield.

1675-   King Philip's War.
1676

1684   Massachusetts loses its charter and becomes a royal colony.

1685   Accession of James II.

1688   "Glorious Revolution" in England.

1689   Accession of William III.

1691   Massachusetts gains new charter but loses many of its former rights.

1699   Creation of Brattle Street Church, Boston.

1701   New college is chartered in Connecticut, eventually to be named Yale.

1702   Publication of Cotton Mather's *Magnalia Christi Americana.*

1723   Death of Increase Mather.

1728   Death of Cotton Mather.

1740-   The Great Awakening.
1742

1758   Death of Jonathan Edwards.

CHAPTER 1

The English Background of Puritanism American

T HE American Puritans were part of a group that had its origins in sixteenth-century England. Some familiarity with the events that led up to the Great Migration to New England in the 1620s and 1630s or at least the shape of these events is necessary for an understanding of Puritanism in America. Quite as important is the intellectual inheritance that the Puritans, as Puritans, brought from England. Since the early Puritans, in both England and New England, were devoted to the "plain style," much of what they had to say is still clear and understandable, though they wrote more than 350 years ago. For this reason and because their language suggests their thought patterns, some of the leading spokesmen for Puritanism, clergymen and laymen, can usefully be allowed to speak for themselves. The use of contemporary documents often has the effect, when modernized slightly, of bringing that which is remote in time a good deal closer.

I *The Beginnings of Puritanism*

By the end of the Middle Ages, many Christians, especially intellectuals, believed that the Christian church had departed from the example provided by the churches of New Testament days. The elaborate ceremonies associated with the Mass and the complicated system of penance were among the developments that appeared to have submerged the simplicity and purity of Christ's Gospel. Among those who advocated reform were such Christian humanists as Thomas More and Erasmus, who sought renovation within the church. Others favored a more radical housecleaning, including a break from the authority of the Pope. In England, Protestant reformers did not achieve dominant influence until the reign of

Edward VI (1547-1553), though the Church of England had been formally separated from Rome in the reign of Edward's father, Henry VIII, and William Tyndale, who was active in Henry's reign, had a considerable influence on later religious thought. Tyndale taught that, in matters of doctrine, the Scriptures were all-sufficient.

Edward's reign was short, and he was succeeded by the Catholic Mary, who re-established the dependence of the English church on Rome. The shaping of the reformed Church of England, begun under Edward, was resumed, after Mary's brief reign, under Queen Elizabeth. At the beginning of Elizabeth's reign two attitudes towards the church can be noted among reformers. Some argued doctrine was all important; if the church taught the truth, then such matters as vestments, ceremonies, and church organization were indifferent. Others, influenced by the practice of the Reformed churches of the Rhineland and Switzerland, as well as by their theology, believed that the church should be thoroughly purified in externals as well as in doctrine. The goal of the queen was the stabilization of the country; it could be effected, she believed, by a comprehensive church that might accommodate both Protestants and conservatives who had been Roman Catholics. Therefore the Church of England taught a form of doctrine that was wholly acceptable to Protestants, while it retained many Catholic traditions, notably what the Protestant John Jewel labelled, scornfully, "the scenic apparatus of divine worship." For a time many reformers believed that the Elizabethan Compromise was only temporary and tentative. It was not, and by the middle of the 1560s controversy arose over the continuing requirement that ministers wear religious vestments while conducting services. Of particular importance was the question: Were the vestments evil because they were consecrated to idolatry through their use in the Mass? Or were they, though indifferent, a proper requirement because they were traditional symbols of status and a means of identification? Those who considered vestments evil were in time called Puritans; those who defended them can be called conservatives. [1]

In time three parties of Protestant reformers existed within the Elizabethan Church of England. One group sought modest reforms, such as the elimination of vestments and more emphasis on preaching, not fundamental changes in the constitution of the Church. Advocates of this position included John Foxe, the martyrologist; Edmund Spenser, the poet; and Edmund Grindal, who became Archbishop of Canterbury. Seeing that attempts at even minor changes were unsuccessful, a second group blamed the episcopal structure that had continued in the Church since pre-Reformation days and urged its destruction. For the hierarchy they would have substituted a system of government by coequal ministers. The governing bodies were to be the ministers meeting together as a "classis." Aggressively led by such men as Thomas Cartwright and John Field, this group first sought change through Parliament but was unsuccessful. Later, in the 1580s, they began to organize conferences of the clergy on a regular basis as a kind of underground government. But they were soon exposed, and the so-called classical movement was destroyed. A third group, which developed in the 1570s, also favored a different church structure, but its members were cautious about how practical reform was to be brought about. Unlike the more revolutionary group, this "spiritual brotherhood" of practical Puritans devoted their efforts to preaching and pastoral care, in the hope that by cultivating the support of the people of their parishes and through passive resistance they could create a large body of lay opinion in favor of change. They practiced nonconformity; that is, they avoided wherever possible what ecclesiastical regulations required when the regulations offended their consciences. This group grew in strength when the efforts of the revolutionary group came to naught, and in the seventeenth century they prepared the way for the English Revolution of the 1640s. Among the important leaders in the sixteenth century were Laurence Chaderton, Richard Greenham, and William Perkins. The Separatists, a fourth group, were so discouraged by the failure of the reform efforts that they withdrew from the Church of England and established separate reformed congregations.[2]

The first three groups, and sometimes the fourth, were called Puritans, without distinction, by their contemporaries. Each group made contributions to literature and thought. The anti-vestment party contributed analyses of the "external" religion, the superstitions, the ceremonies, the immorality and ignorance that they found within the Church. The revolutionaries, in their debates with the conservatives, worked out an intellectual position on such fundamental issues as the source of religious authority and the nature of the Church. This third group, the most successful, included men of caution, conservatism, and compromise. These practical Puritans, especially the Cambridge University intellectuals, produced a massive literature setting forth attitudes towards almost every imaginable subject: the family, the structure of society, morality, education, economics. Later Puritans continued their traditions and inherited this rich literature, which did much to shape their thought. Two Cambridge lecturers and writers of great influence were Thomas Cartwright (1535-1603), the authority on fundamental issues, and William Perkins (1558-1602), the most encyclopedic in his learning.[3]

II *Thomas Cartwright and William Perkins*

Chiefly through his writings, Thomas Cartwright made his reputation as a controversialist. He participated in an extended debate, in print, with John Whitgift, later Archbishop of Canterbury, that focused on the issue: Is the Church of England really what the Christian church should be? The importance of Cartwright's critique of the church is shown by the fact that when Richard Hooker prepared his definitive defense of the English church, he wrote in the context provided by Cartwright's formulations. Cartwright's writings on the Bible and the church also prepared the way for the Congregationalists, as New Englanders such as Richard Mather and John Cotton were to acknowledge.

Cartwright taught, emphasized, insisted, and repeated that the Bible was intended by God to be a perfect statement of how He was to be worshipped and how men were to live. According to Cartwright, "All things pertaining to the kingdom of Heaven, whether in matter of doctrine or government," are set forth in the Bible. "The Lord God, determining to set before our eyes a perfect form of his church, is both able to do it and hath done it." It is natural, thought Cartwright, that God should be so explicit, since it is "the virtue of a good law to leave as little undetermined" as possible. The explicitness of the Old Testament's moral and judicial law is a clear indication of God's mind, and this law is permanent: it was not repealed by the New Testament. Since his opponents shared Cartwright's attitude towards the Bible as a source of doctrine, it was on the subject of worship and church government that he had most to say.[4]

Christian worship is circumscribed and determined, taught Cartwright, by four rules of St. Paul:

1. "that all should not offend any, especially the church of God";
2. "that all be done in order and comeliness";

3. "that all be done to edifying";
4. "that they be done to the glory of God."

Since these laws, if comprehensive, do not specify "the hour and the time and day of prayer, etc.," Cartwright recognized that men may think themselves free to do what they will on matters not determined by the Bible. But he insists that "even those things that are indifferent and may be done have their freedom grounded of the Word of God." For him "it is necessary to have the Word of God go before us in all our actions [because] . . . we cannot otherwise be assured that they please God." Cartwright found three church officers prescribed by Scripture: bishops or pastors, who teach the Word and govern; elders, who do not teach but who assist in the governing; and deacons, who distribute the church's treasure to the poor. The pastors are coequal, there being no hierarchy. Besides preaching, the pastors administer the sacraments and are responsible for the discipline of the church, which includes private admonition, public reproof, and excommunication. Cartwright stressed the importance of church discipline. Since it lacked many of the characteristics set forth in Scripture, he found the Church of England utterly deficient. (But it should be added that Cartwright never actually left the Church.) His emphasis on the Bible as the one sole reliable guide became a central Puritan conviction.[5]

The Cartwrightian view of the church is everywhere implied in the writings of William Perkins. As a lecturer at Cambridge University, Perkins provided a nearly definitive Puritan view of every area of religion and morality except the church. All that Perkins touched he handled methodically and fully. While he took a strongly predestinarian stand (he taught double predestination: election and reprobation), his interest was less in pure theology than in its practical application. The experience of religious conversion had become an increasing concern among the practical Puritan preachers, and Perkins was one of the first English divines to elaborate the structure of the conversion experience. His starting place is Paul's statement, "And those whom he predestined he also called; and those whom he called he also justified; and those whom he justified he also glorified" (Romans 8:30). Perkins amplified this brief statement. The first step, Effectual Calling, he defined as the means "whereby a sinner being severed from the world is entertained unto God's family." Calling or Vocation occurs by "the saving hearing of the Word of God, which is when the said Word outwardly is preached to such a one as is both dead in his sins and doth not so much as dream of salvation." The result is a softening of the otherwise stony heart of him who has been called, and the creation of faith, "a miraculous and supernatural faculty of the heart," by which Christ is received. The second step is Justification: God accounts the believer to be just through Christ's obedience. In this step God remits man's sins and imputes Christ's righteousness to him; by these processes he receives the benefits of Adoption: power to be accounted a son of God. The third step, Sanctification, continues till death. Man is empowered to lead a life in accordance with God's laws.[6]

One question especially dominated Perkins's thinking: How can one know that one has been called? This question became of overwhelming importance in the thought of such Puritan preachers as Thomas Hooker and John Cotton and had much to do with the Antinomian controversy that disrupted the Massachusetts Bay colony in the 1630s. It was taken up again and again by Perkins. He devoted two works to the question: *A Case of Conscience, The Greatest that ever was: how a man may know whether he be the child of God, or no,* and *A Treatise Tending unto a Declaration, whether a Man be in the Estate of Damnation, or in the Estate of Grace.* Perkins's approach is to cite evidences of salvation: one knows that he is saved if he has a "pure, certain, sure, distinct, and particular" knowledge of God's Word; a full knowledge of and sorrow for his sins through careful self-examination; such evidence of sanctification as "good hearing of the Word," comfort in receiving the Sacrament, hatred of sin, and upright walking in one's calling, a sense of God's mercy. This last will flourish in time, after extended Christian experience, so that he has a full assurance of his salvation. Presumably a person who wishes to find himself saved would take steps to create the evidence that Perkins identifies.[7]

Perkins and, after him, many other Puritans, conceived of the life that the Christian was called to lead in an economic context. Not only was the Christian called to salvation; like all men he was also called to perform a secular task. God "doth particularly set apart" men for particular callings, and "every person of every degree, state, sex, or condition without exception must have some personal and particular calling to walk in." This calling demands devotions and diligence, but one who applies himself seriously to his task can expect to prosper. Perkins's brand of Christianity was very much in sympathy with the ideals of the rising middle class, and this connection led to the popularization of Puritanism among people of energy and ability. Perkins thus played an important role in the development of what might be called Puritan capitalism. Puritans frequently expressed shock and disgust that the established church was so involved with politics and political power; but without the strong support of influential men of business, they would not have flourished as they did.[8]

Because of Perkins's interest in vocation, both religious and secular, it was natural that he should discuss preaching, which he considered, like other Puritans, the usual means by which God called men to salvation. The foundation of the central idea of *means* is Paul's statement in Romans 10:17, "Faith cometh by hearing." As usual, Perkins prepared a full analysis of his subject so that his work *The Art of Prophecying* became the definitive treatment of preaching. For Perkins, the preacher begins with a text from Scripture: "The Scripture is the Word of God written in a language fit for the Church by men immediately called to be clerks or secretaries of the Holy Ghost." The text is then divided; that is, the preacher resolves it into doctrines and applications. Since all Biblical texts are for Perkins either Law or Gospel, the preacher must ascertain which he is dealing with. If Law, the preacher describes the disease of sin, but he finds no remedy for it. If Gospel, he teaches what is to be done to escape from sin, and since the Holy Spirit accompanies efficacious preaching, the Spirit provides the means whereby the Gospel can be believed. Perkins identifies the four parts of a sermon:

1. Reading "the text distinctly out of the canonical Scriptures."
2. Giving "the sense and understanding of it being read, by the Scripture itself."
3. Collecting "a few and profitable points of doctrine out of the natural sense."
4. Applying "(if he have the gift) the doctrines rightly collected to the life and manners of men in a simple and plain speech."

John Udall, a contemporary of Perkins, added a fifth part, the reasons for the doctrine. He argued that "every sentence of the holy Scripture containeth in it (at least) one general doctrine." The truth of this doctrine "must needs be acknowledged to be so." To this end the preacher supports it with "examples and testimonies of the Scripture" and "by the force of reason grounded on the same." By means of the reasons the hearer is "thoroughly persuaded of the

truth" of the doctrine. The five-part plan was used again and again
by Puritan preachers (and non-Puritans, too) for many years. Usually preachers found it convenient to set forth several doctrines within
one sermon, each followed by supporting reasons and then that
which became all-important, the applications.[9]

The sermon was intended to communicate a vivid sense of man's
sinfulness and God's mercy. In keeping with Paul's description of
his own preaching in I Corinthians 2:4: "And my speech and my
preaching was not with enticing words of man's wisdom but in
demonstration of the Spirit and of power," both Udall and Perkins
recommended the "plain style," for a long time characteristic of
most Puritan preaching, and since preachers were "the oracles of
God," their style should not be homely. On the other hand, each
sermon should be aimed at the welfare of the least gifted hearer.
Puritans sought to avoid the complex, ornate prose of preachers
such as John Donne, who was usually more successful at art than at
edification. The plain style was a style for preaching, for vocal
preaching, not for the composition of books, though many Puritan
books were books of sermons. The witty and learned style of
Nathaniel Ward's *Simple Cobler of Aggawam in America* shows
what a Puritan preacher could do when he was not preparing a sermon.[10]

III   *William Ames*

William Perkins and Thomas Cartwright were both intellectuals;
both made historically significant contributions to their university,
Cambridge; and English Puritan traditions became closely tied to
Cambridge. The Puritan emphasis on persuasion, on reasons for
doctrines, was heavy, and since ours is an age that identifies devotion to the authority of the Bible with anti-intellectualism, the
priority that Puritans gave to higher education and things of the
mind cannot be emphasized too much. In the last thirty years the
most attractive aspect of Puritanism for its admirers has been its intellectualism, and Puritanism has therefore proved to be of particular interest to intellectual historians. But the Puritans' psy-
chology balanced reason and the understanding with a conviction
that the will and the heart were equally important. It was a change
of heart that the Puritan preacher sought to bring about. The works
of William Ames (1576 -1633), probably the theologian most influential in seventeenth-century New England, reveal this double

emphasis. Cotton Mather made the point when he noted Ames's rare combination of "a scholastical wit joined with a heart warm in religion."[11]

At Christ's College, Cambridge, Ames studied with Perkins, whose teaching he acknowledged. When the militancy of his Puritanism made it impossible for him to hold a ministerial position in England, Ames crossed the North Sea to Holland, as had a number of like-minded men. There he took part in the debate between Calvinists and Arminians about the conversion process and distinguished himself by the attention he gave to man's role. As professor of theology at the University of Franeker, he wrote a great many books, the most influential of which were *The Marrow of Theology* (1623) and *Conscience* (1630). Both were originally composed in Latin but were later translated into English. The *Marrow*, addressed to laymen but used in educating future ministers, is a compendium designed to provide brief explanations of all the most vital theological matters. *Conscience* supplies concise answers to the most important moral questions of the day. Ames's plans to join the Massachusetts Bay colonists were terminated by death, but his books came in his place. Thomas Hooker, the great New Englander, who had known him in Holland and had contributed a preface to a posthumous work, said, "If a scholar was but well studied in Dr. Ames his *Medula Theologiae* and *Casus Conscientia*, they would make him (supposing him versed in the Scriptures) a good divine, though he had no more books in the world."[12]

The importance Ames gives to piety is shown in his definition of theology in the *Marrow:* "the doctrine of living to God." "Since living is the noblest work of all, there cannot be any more proper study than the art of living." Having established the boundaries of theology, Ames begins its systematic treatment, not with "God and His Essence," but, in keeping with his humanistic concern, with faith. For him faith is an act of both understanding and will, but the grace that produces faith has the will as its "proper and prime subject." Ames's contribution to theology was in reaction to the extreme intellectualism of contemporary Continental orthodoxy, the High Calvinism adopted by the Synod of Dort (1619). That body taught the importance of the decrees of God. In contrast, Ames devotes a chapter of the *Marrow* and a chapter in *Conscience* to man's love of God. The pietistic basis of his theology has led to his being called an empirical theologian. It also suggests Ames's debt to Peter Ramus, whom he called "the greatest master of the arts."[13]

Peter Ramus (1515 - 1572), a French Huguenot philosopher, held
that the proper concern of theology is faith in God and acts of faith,
and, rather like Ames, he defined theology as "the doctrine of living
well." Ramus influenced Ames (and through him and after him,
American Puritans) in another important area. It was Ramus who
popularized dichotomies, or division by two, and Ames, who wrote
two Ramesian logics, used the dichotomy as the framework of his
theological writings. Thus for him God's efficiency is either common or special; special providence consists of man's fall and man's
restoration; man's restoration is redemption by Christ and application of redemption; redemption by Christ is by his person and his
office. This system of analysis can be found in many Puritan
treatises, especially in the emphasis on method and in the form of
"disjunctive axioms." A disjunctive axiom distinguishes what op-
tions are available: the Bible was written by God or it was not; the
devil exists or he does not.[14]

In addition to his empirical approach to theology and his attention to method, Ames is historically important because of his influential teachings on the church, which might be labelled proto-
Congregational. Ames follows St. Augustine in distinguishing
between the invisible church (the institution of which all those
elected for salvation—whether living, dead, or to be born—are
members) and the visible church (the properly organized
ecclesiastical institution of this world, whose members are not
necessarily all elect). He found the visible church to exist as congregations, and he defined a particular church, the unit with which
he is concerned, as "a society of believers joined together in a
special bond for the continual exercise of the communion of saints
among themselves." This special bond is "a covenant, expressed or
implicit, by which believers bind themselves individually to perform all those duties towards God and towards one another which
relate to the purposes of the church and its edification." Ames
equates "edification" and "the communion of the saints." Both
may be described as the interaction of church members with one
another and with Christ, the church being the body of Christ. For
Ames a central passage in the Bible seems to have been Ephesians
4:16, which describes how the church, "fitly joined together and
compacted by that which every joint supplieth, according to the
effectual working in the measure of every part, maketh increase of
the body unto the edifying of itself in love."[15]

The church, the particular church, is for Ames the fundamental Christian body, really the only Christian body. Its members have the right to call their own minister and to effect excommunication. Ames's emphasis on the power of the congregation naturally requires him to discuss the question of separatism. Since most English congregations did not have the power to select their own minister and none of them to exercise the power of excommunication, should Christians withdraw from such imperfect churches? Ames offers several arguments *against* separation. It is "lawful to continue in that church where the power of removing scandal and purging out the wicked is wanting." It is "lawful to stay in such a church where some of the ordinances of Christ are wanting" because "an imperfection . . . doth not take away the nature of that office which is found more perfect in some persons or state." Ames was not a thorough-going radical, and his variety of Puritanism retained certain Christian traditions from his mildly conservative bias.[16]

Ames identified the ordinary ministers of the church as "pastors and teachers or ruling elders," and he argued that ordination of a minister without a title, that is, without a church in which he is to serve, is "as ridiculous as trying to imagine a husband without a wife." How effective these declarations were is shown by John Cotton's explanation of how Congregationalism originated: "The particular visible church of a congregation to be the first subject of the power of the keys [that is, the power to choose officers, partake of the sacrament, and censure offenders], we received by the light of the Word from Mr. [Robert] Parker, Mr. [Paul] Baynes, and Dr. Ames."[17]

IV   *The Growth of Puritanism*

In Elizabeth's reign the important areas of difference between Puritans and conservatives did not include doctrine. Both shared the Reformed theology of Calvin and his fellows, such as Martin Bucer, Heinrich Bullinger, and Peter Martyr. The Thirty-Nine Articles, the Church of England's official statement of doctrine, taught predestination. Calvin's catechism was in use at Oxford and Cambridge, and his influence was strong. As time passed it became easier for the Puritans to retain their Calvinist theology than for those who accepted the Church establishment, since most Puritans considered the Reformed churches of the Continent to be models

that the Church of England should emulate. Though the theology
of the New England Puritans included the special features of Covenant Theology, they considered themselves, properly, to be
Calvinists as late as Cotton Mather's time and beyond. On the other
hand, in the early seventeenth century there developed among non-
reformist Anglicans a new school of theology. This school, the High
Church party, sought to find a theological middle way between
Protestantism and Catholicism. They emphasized not God's decrees
or the conversion process but episcopacy's authority in church
government and the sacramental and esthetic aspects of religion in
worship. Because Parliament was hostile to their position and King
Charles was sympathetic, they emphasized the royal authority in
church affairs. Consequently, the separation between church
leaders and Puritans increased, especially after William Laud, one
of the High Churchmen, came into power. This development occurred about the same time as the debate between Arminians and
Calvinists on the Continent (the Arminians taught that man could
accept or reject God's grace if it were offered to him), and a
polarization ensued. Many Puritans felt obliged to reassert their
loyalty to strict Reformed orthodoxy.[18]

The newly and more rigidly defined orthodoxy of the Canons of
the Synod of Dort embraced five points:

1. Predestination. All men by justice merit punishment for their part in
the sin of Adam, but God provides mercy for some through Christ. The
elect, "though by nature neither better nor more deserving than others . . .
God has decreed to give to Christ to be saved by him." The elect are called
by the ministry of the Word to Christ, and are given faith, which "proceeds
from God's eternal decree." Those who do not believe are the reprobate.
God has decreed that they should be left to their just condemnation, for
"the cause or guilt of this unbelief . . . is nowise in God, but in man
himself."
2. Limited atonement. "It was the will of God Christ by the blood of the
cross . . . should effectually redeem out of every people, tribe, nation, and
language, all those and those only who were from eternity chosen to salvation and given to him by the Father. . . . This purpose, proceeding from
everlasting love towards the elect, has from the beginning of the world to
this day been powerfully accomplished. . . ."
3. Total depravity. Man is totally depraved, unable to perform any saving good, unable to reform.
4. Irresistible grace. Regeneration is "nowise effected by the external
preaching of the gospel, by moral suasion, or such mode of operation that,
after God has performed his part, it still remains in the power of man to be

regenerated or not, to be converted or remain unconverted; but it is at the same time evidently a supernatural work, most powerful and at the same time most delightful, astonishing, mysterious, and ineffable, not inferior in efficacy to creation or the resurrection from the dead . . . so that all in whose hearts God works in this marvelous manner are certainly, infallibly, and effectually regenerated, and do actually believe."

—— 5. Perseverance of the saints. Those whom God calls to salvation, he confirms and they persevere to the end. These have assurance of salvation according to the measure of their faith. "This certainty of perseverance . . . should serve as an incentive to the serious and constant practice of good works. . . ."

The "five points" had a special place in Puritan thought. They were the tests of orthodoxy. These doctrines were assumptions often taken up by Puritan preachers, who were, however, seldom interested in academic theology. Their concern was *application*.[19]

It may be difficult to conceive that these beliefs of man could have much popular appeal. A helpful explanation has been provided by William Haller: "The concept of universal depravity, by leveling all superiority not of the spirit, enormously enhanced the self-respect of the ordinary man. If none were righteous, then one man was as good as another. God chose whom he would and the distinctions of this world counted for nothing. . . . over against the aristocracy which ruled the world, there was an aristocracy of the spirit, chosen by God and destined to inherit heaven and earth."[20]

In the years 1610 - 1640 there were a good many reasons for being a Puritan. A few that may be specified were especially important. (1) Many effective teachers at Cambridge University during the years 1580 - 1615 were Puritans, and they produced large numbers of effective Puritan ministers. At Trinity, St. John's, and particularly Christ's and Emanuel Colleges Puritanism was strong, and graduates of these colleges in large numbers went out with enthusiasm to teach and preach Puritan values. These ministers were idealists who devoted themselves to preaching and pastoral care, very different from the opportunistic careerists, who accepted the Church and did not press for reform. (2) Puritan concern with discipline in the Church led to an identification of Puritanism with high moral standards and with law and order. Something of this relationship can be seen from Lucy Hutchinson's contemporary account of how the name "Puritan" came to be used: "Whoever was zealous for God's glory or worship, could not endure blasphemous oaths, ribald conversation, profane scoffs, sabbath-breaking, derision of the Word of God, and the like—whoever could endure a sermon, modest habit, or conversation, or anything good—all these were Puritans."[21]

(3) There were many nonreligious reasons for being a Puritan. For example, the Puritans opposed the traditional observation of saints' days and taught that the Sabbath should be kept holy. This program was in keeping with the capitalist need for a regular work week. Similarly, the teachings of men such as Perkins on vocation appealed to those who benefitted from the employment of industrious workers. (4) The Church of England suffered from the poor quality of bishops appointed by King James in the early part of the seventeenth century. Most of them were worldly politicians at best, and they were on the whole quite indifferent to the religious needs of the Church. (5) Englishmen reacted strongly against the growth of Roman Catholicism at the royal court in the 1620s and 1630s. Catholicism was identified with England's historic enemies, France and Spain. The Puritans, who were strongly anti-Roman Catholic (it was "the remnants of Romanism" that they sought to remove from the English church), benefitted greatly from the anti-Catholic reaction. (6) As the bishops looked to the king who had appointed them for support and as the king looked to the bishops to preach the royal prerogative, those in the House of Commons who were unhappy with the extent of the royal authority looked to the Puritans for support. Thus two parties developed—the Court party and the party of Parliamentarians and Puritans. Because Puritanism was a reform movement that provided a radical criticism of the whole established order, including the social structure, it attracted men who sought fundamental changes in that structure. It attracted and it created revolutionaries, but its devotion to morality and order drew conservatives as well. The English revolution of the 1640s was more than a Puritan revolution, but it was under the banner of Puritanism that many men marched.[22]

The conservative tendency can be seen in the Puritan reaction to the work of William Laud. As Bishop of London (1628) and later as Archbishop of Canterbury (1633), Laud became the most powerful man in the government of Charles I. His opposition to Puritanism took two forms. First, he brought into new prominence the ceremonial and external aspects of religion that the Puritans found most objectionable. Laud's own comment on his role puts it in the best light: "Ever since I came in place, I labored nothing more than that the external public worship of God (too much slighted in most parts of this kingdom) might be preserved, and that with as much decency and uniformity as might be, being still of opinion that unity cannot long continue in the Church where uniformity is shut out at the Church door." Laud treated the communion table as an altar and ordered that it be moved to the east end in each church; he insisted that churches be consecrated; he enforced regulations, previously much ignored, that required bowing to the altar; he restored the stained glass windows in the chapel at Lambeth Palace—in short, he emphasized the Anglo-Catholic ideal of the beauty of holiness. At the same time he campaigned to stop or at least limit the Puritan lecturers—ministers without church posts who preached in London and other market towns, often with large followings. (These popular preachers were usually paid from funds raised locally to provide more preaching.) In a variety of ways Laud sought to eliminate nonconformity within the Church.[23]

The Puritan perception of Laud is set forth in the *Articles Exhibited Against William Archbishop of Canterbury, 1640.* Among them are these: (VII) "That by false enormious [sic] doctrines and other sinister ways and means he went about to subvert the religion established in this kingdom and to set up Papistry and superstition in the Church." (VIII) "That by undue means and practice he hath gotten into his hand the power of nominating ministers thereunto, and that he preferred corrupt chaplains to his majesty." (XI) "That to suppress preaching he hath suspended divers good men and used unlawful means by letters and otherwise to several bishops, to suppress them." Here conservatives speak against an innovator. Laud's campaign in the long run was not a success (indeed, it brought about his personal downfall), but for a time it was a serious threat to Puritanism. The movement to America was substantially encouraged by Laudian oppression.[24]

V   *The Puritan Migration*

With this account of Puritan thought and experience as background, it is now time to turn to those who were to become American Puritans. Secular-minded historians and Marxists are wont to argue that Puritanism had little to do with the beginnings of New England. Just as there were nonreligious reasons for being a Puritan, so there were admittedly several nonreligious reasons for leaving England. In the early years of the seventeenth century the old agrarian society disintegrated. The capitalist society that replaced it suffered in the beginning severe dislocations: economic depression marked the years 1619 - 1624, 1629 - 1631, and 1637 - 1640. There were plague years too, and bad harvests. In the strongly Puritan area of East Anglia, economic conditions reached crisis levels in 1629.[25]

Therefore thousands of Englishmen left their country. Some went to the Continent, some to the Caribbean, some to North America. About eighty thousand people, or about two percent of the population, left England between 1620 and 1642. Many Englishmen believed that their country was suffering from overpopulation, and the new colonies that were opened up enjoyed favorable publicity from propagandists. Captain John Smith, for example, propagandized diligently for colonization of America during three decades. Smith preached the satisfactions of being one's own master in a land of unlimited opportunity. He was no Puritan.[26]

The political situation in England in the 1620s and 1630s was another reason why some men sought to leave England. Soon after Charles I came to the throne he issued, in 1626, a letter to religious and secular leaders "to require and collect a loan for the King's use from persons able to lend." This letter, issued for what Charles called "reasons of state," infringed on the prerogatives of Parliament, and many men refused to furnish the money demanded. Among those who resisted the so-called benevolence and were consequently imprisoned were the Earl of Lincoln, a central figure in the creation of the Massachusetts Bay Company; Samuel Vassal and William Spurstow, who were among the original members of the Company; and William Coddington, who came to Massachusetts in 1630. This incident was only one of many that persuaded Englishmen, especially those sympathetic to Parliament and Puritanism, that the king was exceeding the proper limits of royal power. A constitutional crisis was clearly in the making.[27]

Such conditions as these had much to do with the creation of the Massachusetts Bay Company. On the other hand, most, if not all, of its leaders were demonstrably Puritans, and it was at least in the name of religion that they left England. Those who wrote back to England from America argued that the only valid reason for migrating to Massachusetts was religion. Circumstances had provided Puritans with what their ministers later called "an open door of liberty" to establish true churches. Puritan clergymen in England urged their congregations to migrate to a place where they could practice their religion in a pure church, and those who wrote back to England in the first decade to describe what they found in the Bay colony emphasized how important the establishment of Puritan churches was in the new land.[28]

In the creation of the Massachusetts Bay Company, the organization that undertook the migration to New England in 1629 and after, the existence of the Plymouth colony, created in 1620, seems to have been of small importance, though the new arrivals at Massachusetts Bay benefitted greatly from the near proximity of fellow Englishmen when the younger colony was established. The Plymouth men traded with the new arrivals and provided much-needed advice on a variety of subjects. The Plymouth colonists who had reached the New World in 1620 were a mixed group. Of the 102 who crossed the sea on the *Mayflower*, half were "saints" and half "strangers": a nucleus of English Separatists whose history went back to the beginning of the century, and a collection of individuals whose interests in migration had nothing to do with religion. The Separatists, or Pilgrims, had lived for some dozen years in Holland, where they could practice their religion, but they were not happy there. William Bradford, one of their leaders, recorded why they left for America. Life was hard in Holland. They could scarcely make a living. Their children were in danger of corruption from the low morality that prevailed among the Dutch they lived with, and they were afraid of losing their English identity. Moreover, they had "a great hope and inward zeal . . . of laying some good foundation . . . for the propagation and advancing the gospel of the kingdom of Christ in these remote parts of the world."[29]

The Massachusetts Bay Company settlers had stronger backing than the small and poor Plymouth group, though both suffered greatly and lost large numbers through death during the founding of the new settlements. The Massachusetts Bay Company came into existence from a modest base, the Dorchester Company of Adventurers, who established a small plantation (as such settlements were regularly called) at Cape Ann, Massachusetts, in 1623. The Dorchester Company's property was later transferred to the New England Company, which sent a group of fifty to join what was left of the earlier body of men. More men and women came over in 1629, and they established at Salem the first church in the new colony. With a new royal charter to the land, the first large group of settlers, nearly a thousand, arrived in 1630, and by 1642 some twenty thousand people had migrated to New England.[30]

The leaders of the 1628 group were officially informed that "the propagation of the Gospel is the thing we do profess above all to be our aim in settling this plantation," and they were told that care had been taken to purge all "libertines" from the early migrants. The same letter reports that the first ministers of the new colony have "declared themselves to be of one judgment and to be fully agreed on the manner how to exercise their ministry." The ministers, Samuel Skelton and Francis Higginson, were both Puritans. More specifically, they were believers in the Congregational way of church organization. Most of those who came later had been sufficiently influenced by William Ames and Thomas Hooker that they were at least inclined towards the Congregational way.[31]

VI *John Winthrop*

Of the laymen associated with the beginnings of the Massachusetts Bay colony, the fullest surviving records concern John Winthrop, the first governor of the colony and its leading civil leader for nearly twenty years. In 1629 he prepared a widely circulated paper that sets forth eight "Arguments for the Plantation of New England." Winthrop cites both economic considerations (overpopulation and the possibility of prosperity in the New World) and religious-moral reasons, but the latter loom larger. He notes the possibility of missionary work, the opportunity to provide a refuge for those whom God intends to save from the general destruction that seemed to threaten European and English churches, the need to escape from the intemperance that he found to be overwhelming society. Two particularly Puritan reasons are worth noting fully. He fears for his children: "The fountains of learning and religion are so corrupted as besides the unsupportable charge of their education, even the best wits and fairest hopes are perverted, corrupted, and utterly overthrown by the multitude of evil examples and the licentious government of those seminaries." The influence that Puritanism had enjoyed at Cambridge University was largely a thing of the past there by the late 1620s. Winthrop also cited a particularly Congregational concern: "What can be a better work and more honorable and worthy a Christian than to help raise and support a particular church while it is in its infancy and to join our forces with such a company of faithful people. . . ?" The New England adventure offered the possibility of joining with a group of like-minded Puritans, Congregational Puritans, who planned to establish a pure church in the new land, far away from the immorality that was so threatening to Winthrop in the England of his time.[32]

The basis of Winthrop's intense Puritanism was a conversion experience he set forth in a spiritual autobiography in 1636. Entitled "Relation of His Religious Experience," it provides a valuable insight into the emotional state that drove Puritans into undertakings as hazardous as the Massachusetts Bay experiment. Winthrop explains that as a boy he was little interested in religion and was full of wickedness (probably an overstatement, but Winthrop's whole report is highly subjective). At about the age of twelve he read some religious books and became somewhat restrained. In his middle teens while he was a student at Cambridge University, he was for a time ill and isolated, and in reaction he turned to God, but only for a time, until his health improved. Then once again he neglected God and became worse than ever, though he experienced occasional good moods.

At the age of eighteen he married and came under the influence of the Reverend Ezekiel Culverwell, who preached near his wife's home. A well-known Puritan preacher, Culverwell had been suspended at one time for not wearing the surplice. Through the minister's influence Winthrop became much attached to religion and sermons. He established a reputation for himself as a very devout man, and many resorted to him for religious advice. He even thought that he should enter the ministry. All this time he did not, he wrote, seriously question his state to see if he was among the elect. Then he read in the writings of William Perkins that reprobates could do as much as he had done and that he had no occasion to consider himself saved. He now knew how totally depraved he was, that he was really a hypocrite in matters of religion. He tried desperately to "lay hold upon Christ in some promise" made in the Bible, but he could not. All that he could do was to make a strenuous effort to avoid sin. He found himself constantly troubled, not so much for fear that he would be damned but because he lacked assurance of salvation.

For a long time Winthrop remained, by his account, very devout but very uncomfortable. Finally at about the age of thirty he began to have a greater understanding of religion. Now God afflicted him sorely, and he knew fully and completely his unworthiness. Finally from this depth he was lifted up, and "every promise I thought upon held forth Christ unto me, saying, 'I am thy salvation.'" From this conversion experience he could detect the mortification

of his corruptions and "the new man quickened." Winthrop
became aware of Christ's constant presence. Though in time he did
experience periods of spiritual dullness, he was always drawn back
to God and to a realization of his ingratitude. The flesh and the
spirit continued to war within him, and he experienced many falls
"through dead-heartedness," but he found from then on that he
was always raised up again.[33]

Obviously the central religious question was for Winthrop, What
is my relationship to God? His doubts, his struggles within himself,
his profound anxiety, his conviction of his depravity and unworthiness—all of these are characteristic of the Puritan religious
experience as described by those who suffered through it and by
those—the preachers such as Thomas Hooker—who described it in
quite as full detail. Winthrop's ultimate awareness of sanctification
and assurance, despite lapses, is, like his earlier experiences, wholly
private and inner, a matter of the heart. Though Puritanism, especially the Congregational variety, made much of the communion
of the saints in church fellowship, and though it has been said that
no place in man's history has given greater primacy to the intellect
than Puritan New England, the religious experience of the Puritan
was that of the lonely, separate soul.

CHAPTER 2

The Puritan Fathers of New England

PERHAPS as many as twenty thousand people moved to New England during the first dozen years of the Massachusetts Bay colony, 1630 - 1642, after which the turn of political events in England encouraged Puritans to stay at home. All of those who migrated were not Puritans, but the most careful studies suggest that religious motivation was a significant factor. New England's Puritanism early became famous, and those not attracted to it could go elsewhere, to the Caribbean or to Virginia.[1]

Those who ventured came mostly as part of a family group, typically a husband and a wife in their thirties or forties, a few children, and one or more servants. The men were solid citizens, mainly farmers and craftsmen; few really poor people came. They were from many parts of England, united chiefly in their devotion to local control, in opposition to the meddling of bishops and royal officials and tax collectors, for these were years when King Charles was attempting to expand both his civil and his ecclesiastical authority. The interests of most Englishmen were local, and the kind of people who emigrated were accustomed to running their own communities.[2]

In New England these people practiced local control. The government they developed was chiefly what we now call the New England town meeting system, and their churches were directed by the local congregation. Each town came to have its own character, but each attempted to avoid outside control by creating harmony within, usually by means of carefully defined town covenants and church covenants. Naturally in such an atmosphere, the colony's federal government had some difficulties in attempting to deal with matters of broad concern such as taxation.[3]

Although the seventeenth century was a period of great unrest everywhere in Europe, in New England harmony prevailed until

late in the century. Some commentators have gone so far as to label
social cohesion in Massachusetts "the Puritans' greatest
achievement." Puritanism itself was the binding force, for it was
widely accepted. Those who were unsympathetic were not merely
discouraged from settling; they were denied the opportunity by
laws that gave town officials the right to determine who might settle
there. Massachusetts Bay Congregationalism permitted some flex-
ibility, some variety of opinion, but a sense of what was orthodox
became well established. One way of handling dissent was through
public debate, with orthodoxy supported by vigorous and effective
champions. Potential troublemakers were soon facing a strong
religious tradition, even though Congregationalism itself was
worked out on Massachusetts soil.[4]

I Bradford and the Plymouth Colony

Their descendants and their successors have venerated the first
generation in New England—the Puritan Fathers—for their
bravery and their idealism. For a long time those who came after
them believed that the founders had held the truth in all its pristine
glory. Whether a religious decline really took place in the late
seventeenth century has been debated, but the tradition established
by the Fathers was unquestionably of real importance. It is against
the Puritanism of its first generation that later Puritanism has been
measured.[5]

The little colony of Plymouth, absorbed into Massachusetts Bay
in 1692, was never very populous or prosperous, though it came to
occupy a sizeable and attractive piece of what is now the Commonwealth of Massachusetts. Its importance in American history
rests on the assistance it gave to the settlers to the north and on the
heroism of its founders. The memory of the struggles of the Pilgrims
in the 1620s has been kept green by the greatest book from
seventeenth-century America, *Of Plymouth Plantation*, written by
its best historian, William Bradford. Bradford's history was well
known from as early as 1669, when his nephew, Nathaniel Morton,
published *New Englands Memoriall*, written largely on the basis of
the older man's book. Not published until 1856, *Of Plymouth Plantation* was used by later historians in the colonial period. Many
drew on it heavily.[6]

Bradford began his history by explaining his tradition. (This topic
he also explored, at some length, in "A Dialogue, or the sum of a

Conference Between Some Young Men Born in New England and Sundry Ancient Men That Came Out of Holland and Old England.") For Bradford, the central tenet of his tradition was devotion to church discipline. It was hatred of this "holy discipline of Christ in His church" that led, according to Bradford, to the persecution of the Puritans in the early years of Elizabeth's reign. Because they were unable to practice their discipline within the Church of England, some Puritans "joined themselves (by a covenant of the Lord) into a church estate in the fellowship of the Gospel." These Separatists taught the idea that later developed into Congregationalism, although historically the Congregationalism of the Massachusetts Bay Puritans is not derived from this tradition yet was probably influenced by the Plymouth model. (The Separatist tradition led nowhere—except to New England.) A Separatist, Robert Browne, was the first to develop the view that discipline is an essential mark of the church and that without it no church is true. For Browne, the true church was the church of the committed, and discipline was required to separate from the church both the uncommitted and those whose lives were inconsistent with their commitment.[7]

One truly committed group was Bradford's. At Scrooby, Nottinghamshire, near the center of England, they gathered in the early years of the seventeenth century. Under the leadership of William Brewster, a layman, they obtained as pastor a Church of England clergyman, John Smith, who had left the Church. Soon they had a second minister, the Reverend John Robinson, who became the spiritual leader of the group, though he did not reach America. After a year of church fellowship, government officials heard about the illegal church and set about to destroy it. Brewster and others were heavily fined. It became clear to church members that they would have to leave England in order to maintain their identity.[8]

While Bradford's group had withdrawn from the Church of England and was officially Separatist and the Puritans of Massachusetts Bay were not, ideologically the two were very close. What distinguished the two groups, their relationship to the Church of England, had been meaningful in England and also on the Continent, but when both were in America it was largely a matter of history that distinguished them—and social class. Even before the Pilgrims came to America they had begun to abandon strict Separatism, and Bradford wrote in his "Dialogue" that he found no important differences between the church of his tradition and the Massachusetts Bay churches. He noted that the Plymouth church had *separated* from the corruptions of the Church of England, whereas the Bay churches had *seceded* from the same corruptions. The churches of the two colonies early established fellowship, and in time Harvard-trained ministers, including John Cotton's son, settled in the Plymouth colony.[9]

Bradford's view of history rests on an understanding of how God acts in human history; his historiography is providential in vision. Providential history is of course Biblical, but for the Puritans the immediate inspiration was John Foxe's immensely popular and influential *Actes and Monuments,* usually called "The Book of Martyrs," a book that Bradford cites. The heroes of the resolutely Protestant Foxe were the Marian martyrs. The lives, deeds, and deaths of the Protestants under England's Catholic Queen Mary served as a model for the Puritans, and especially the Separatists, in two significant ways. First, Foxe pictures the martyrs, in William Haller's words, as "setting the example and defining the themes of discourse to be followed by the swarm of preachers who sprang up under Elizabeth and supplied the inspiration and energy behind the Puritan movement." Second, Foxe's picture of an illegal underground church—in London, during Mary's reign—provided the Separatists with a model and the beginnings of a tradition. (Bradford cites this church as the archetypical Separatist church.)[10]

More generally, Foxe saw the events of the Reformation and especially the English Reformation as the work of God's will. The climax of Christian history was to be reached in English history. In the seventeenth century through the influence of Foxe's providential interpretation, the American Puritans saw themselves to be God's instruments as they first suffered persecution and then escaped from the corruptions of the Church of England to create pure churches in the American wilderness. Thus Cotton Mather began his *Magnalia Christi Americana* (published in 1702, but written a few years earlier):

I write the wonders of the Christian religion, flying from the depravations of Europe, to the American strand; and assisted by the Holy Author of that religion, I do with all conscience of truth, required therein by Him, who is the truth itself, report the wonderful displays of His infinite power, wisdom, goodness, and faithfulness, wherewith his divine providence hath irradiated an Indian wilderness.

Bradford was convinced that God's providence was the explanation
for the Pilgrims' exodus out of England, where the Church was corrupted by "base and beggarly ceremonies" of "men's invention."[11]

Bradford's Pilgrims left England for Holland because their
desires "were set on the ways of God and to enjoy His ordinances."
To achieve this end, "they rested on his providence," and
providence in turn led them to New England. During their voyage
and throughout their early years in America Bradford could detect
God's activities. In his account of their ocean crossing Bradford
wrote that "I may not omit here a special work of God's
providence." A "profane young man," one of the seamen, cursed
and denounced the Pilgrims, but God smote him, he became sick,
and he died. Another young man fell into the sea, but he was a
Pilgrim, and he was rescued. Once they landed, God's providence
was immediately made known, for they came across Indian corn, "a
special providence of God and a great mercy to His poor people,"
which provided "seed to plant their corn for the next year, or else
they might have starved." When they were attacked by Indians, "it
pleased God to vanquish their enemies and give them deliverance,
and by His special providence so to dispose that not any one of
them were either hurt or hit." Later an Indian came to their aid;
Squanto became their interpreter and was "a special instrument
sent of God for their good beyond their expectations."[12]

Bradford wrote his history over a period of years. He began it in
1630, the year the first large group of migrants came to New
England. He saw the first ten years (1620 - 1630) with the eyes of
one who believed that God had used the men of Plymouth in a
peculiar and immensely important way. He could now see that his
poor Pilgrims had been "stepping stones unto others for the perfor-
ming of so great a work" as "the propagation of the Gospel of the
kingdom of Christ in the remote parts of the world." He believed
that God's plan was being made manifest: the men of Plymouth
were holy instruments for the perfecting of the Reformation that
Bradford had described in the first pages of his history.

The Pilgrims had helped the new arrivals in many ways. One of
the most striking evidences, for Bradford, of God's providence was
the way in which the Plymouth churches had been able to help the
Massachusetts Bay men erect new churches. John Endecott, leader
of the Salem group that came over in 1628, wrote to Plymouth for
medical assistance when disease was plaguing his men. Plymouth
sent Samuel Fuller, who both practiced medicine and served as a

deacon in the Plymouth church. While in Salem, Fuller showed the Salemites how to establish a Congregational church. (They were already inclined towards the Congregational way.) Bradford provides little information about what Fuller did, though he does quote a letter from Endecott, who wrote, "I acknowledge myself much bound to you for your kind love and care in sending Mr. Fuller among us, and rejoice much that I am by him satisfied touching your judgment of the outward form of God's worship." (Bradford also quotes, seemingly with approval, a long account of how the Salem church elected and ordained its ministers in Congregational style.) Other evidence of Fuller's influence is more emphatic. William Hubbard, Congregational minister of Salem's neighboring town, Ipswich, writing about 1680, put it this way: "Concerning the way and manner of their first covenanting together and entering into church fellowship one with another, . . . there is no small appearance that in whole or in part" the Salemites did "receive their platform of church order from those of New Plymouth." Edward Winslow wrote in 1646 that "some of the chief of them [of Massachusetts Bay] advised with us [of Plymouth] . . . how they should fall upon a right platform of worship." Bradford saw the creation of this new church at Salem and the subsequent gathering of later Congregational churches of Massachusetts Bay after Salem's example as a part of a continuing action of God that began with the coming of the Pilgrims to America: "Thus out of small beginnings greater things have been produced by His hand that made all things out of nothing, and gives being to all things that are, and as one small candle may light a thousand, so the light kindled here hath shone unto many, yea in some sort of our whole nation; let the glorious name of Jehovah have all the praise." [13]

Bradford believed that God had brought the Pilgrims to America to establish the true religion and to show the way for larger groups, whose example, he believed, could be the beginning of a much larger and more thorough reformation of the church. But after 1632 Bradford saw fewer and fewer signs of God's providence at work in the colony, and his history falters as a result. For a time man's depravity becomes his theme, and finally, Bradford stopped writing—not because he lacked energy or time, for he began the study of Hebrew in his old age. He stopped, it seems, from lack of motivation. His vision had faded; he could no longer see God at work.

What had happened? Bradford offered a kind of explanation:

men had become greedy, and their greed had separated them from
God and Christian fellowship:

. . . the people of the plantation began to grow in their outward estates, by
reason of the flowing of many people into the country, especially into the
Bay of Massachusetts. By which means corn and cattle rose to a great price,
by which many were much enriched and commodities grew plentiful. And
yet in other regards this benefit turned to their hurt, and this accession of
strength to their weakness. For now as their stocks increased and the increase vendible, *there was no longer holding them together,* but now they
must of necessity go to their great lots. They could not otherwise keep their
cattle, and having oxen grown they must have land for plowing and tillage.
And no man now thought he could keep alive except he had cattle and a
great deal of ground to keep them, all striving to increase their stocks. By
which means they were all scattered all over the Bay [Plymouth Harbor]
quickly and the town *in which they lived compactly till now* was left very
thin and in a short time almost desolate. And if this had been all, it had
been less, though not too much; but the church must also be divided, and
*those that had lived so long together in Christian and comfortable
fellowship must now part and suffer many divisions* [emphasis added].

Some of the Pilgrims dispersed to Duxbury and others went elsewhere, "under one pretense or other, thinking their own conceived
necessity and the example of others a warrant sufficient for them."
"And this I fear," wrote Bradford, "will be the ruin of New
England, at least of the churches of God there, and will provoke the
Lord's displeasure against them." Bradford was probably thinking
of a letter from John Robinson that he had included earlier in his
history. Here the Pilgrims' pastor, who is held up as an ideal of the
faithful shepherd, describes the bond of the covenant in very strong
language: "We are knit together as a body in a most strict and
sacred bond and covenant of the Lord, of the violation whereof we
make great conscience, and by virtue whereof we do hold ourselves
straitly tied to all care of each other's good and of the whole, by
every one and mutually." Opposite the passage Bradford wrote,
much later, a painful protest that now the bond was "decayed and
untied." [14]
From the beginning of his history Bradford had identified the
human heart as the battleground of the war between God and
Satan. Satan triumphs and men fail when they trust in their own
strength. Bradford's book is dominated by human infirmity:
covetousness, poor judgment, cowardice. Through this world the
faithful man travels in humility, and Bradford's people "knew they

were Pilgrims." When they arrived at Cape Cod, their plight was
desperate. Bradford pictured the wilderness that faced them; it was
winter and "all things stand . . . with a weatherbeaten face, and
the whole country, full of woods and thickets. . . ." The only inhabitants were "savage barbarians," and behind the Pilgrims the
"mighty ocean" separated them from their friends. But in their
humility, as they recognized their condition, there was strength.
"What could now sustain them but the Spirit of God and His grace?
May not and ought not the children of these fathers rightly say,
'Our fathers were Englishmen which came over this great ocean,
and were ready to perish in this wilderness, but they cried unto the
Lord, and He heard their voice and looked on their adversity.' "[15]

This contrast of past and present may suggest one of Bradford's
purposes in writing *Of Plymouth Plantation.* In a time when men's
private interests were supplanting the concern for the common
good, Bradford held up the virtues of the earlier Separatists for the
contemplation of the younger generation. Just as in his dialogues, in
which young men question the old, Bradford wrote his history to
memorialize the piety, the holiness of those who had departed. His
particular heroes were John Robinson and William Brewster, of
whom he wrote biographies, of Robinson in Chapter 3 of Book I, of
Brewster in the annal for 1643 in Book II. From time to time Bradford addressed his intended readers directly and exhorted the
"children" to "see with what difficulties their fathers wrestled in
going through these things in their first beginnings; and how God
brought them along, notwithstanding all their weakness and infir-
mities." Then he adds, "As also that some use may be made in after
times by others in such weighty employments." As Bradford's disappointment grew with the failure of the Plymouth colony to maintain its sense of community, so did his insistence on man's sinfulness. Addressing his readers, he suggested what might have been
if men had been more devoted to God and his purposes. His history
is imbued with a spirit of prophecy, much like the historical books
of the Old Testament, and he sought to learn its language, Hebrew,
at the end of his life.[16]

II   *Congregationalism and the Church Covenant*

The Plymouth colony was merely, as Bradford wrote, a small candle shining in the darkness, merely a stepping stone for those to
come afterwards. Those who came after were not in complete agree-

ment as to the reasons for their coming. Thomas Dudley's testimony suggests that the Puritan motives for migration were not very specific. "If any come hither to plant," the deputy governor wrote back to England in 1631, "for worldly ends, that can live well at home, he commits an error, of which he will soon repent, but if for spiritual, and that no particular object hinder his removal [from England], he may find here what may content him." Others who had not Dudley's grim experience of the first winter were more excited at the prospects. John Cotton preached to John Winthrop's departing party in 1630 on a text from II Samuel 7:20: "Moreover, I will appoint a place for my people Israel, and I will plant them that they may dwell in a place of their own and move no more." He found a special providence guiding them in the creation of a new commonwealth, where the saints would have the long-sought ordinances of the church: preaching, discipline, and the sacraments. But despite his text he did not develop the idea of Massachusetts as a new Israel. His chief concern was that the colonists should undertake missionary work with the Indians. John Winthrop's sermon on the *Arbella* on his way to America provided an idea of what the new commonwealth should strive to become: a community knit together to do God's work. It was to be "a city on a hill" to show the world how God's people should live. But only later did Massachusetts men become preoccupied with seeing their efforts in the perspective of world history. Thomas Shepard then saw the colony enjoying "the help of all the former ages and other nations as well as our own, godly and learned divines in them, to take pattern and example from, in the laying of our first foundation both of religion and righteousness, doctrine and discipline, church and commonwealth."[17]

The first spiritual leaders of New England Congregationalism, those who arrived in 1630, included John Wilson, who was expected to serve, with George Phillips, as minister to the large party led by John Winthrop. When this group split up, Wilson became minister of the Boston-Charlestown church. The group that settled at Watertown obtained Phillips's services. The Dorchester settlers, with an organization somewhat apart from the main body of colonists, had two ministers, John Warham and John Maverick. The troublesome Roger Williams arrived the next winter, and late in 1631, John Eliot. The first ministers with established reputations were John Cotton (1584 - 1651) and Thomas Hooker (1586 - 1647). They arrived in September 1633. Cotton became minister, with Wilson, of the

Boston church (there now being a separate church at Charlestown); Hooker became pastor of a congregation at Newtown, later Cambridge. The duties of a Puritan minister were chiefly two: pastoral care and preaching, with the latter especially emphasized, since the preaching of the Word was considered the chief means of grace, of salvation. A New England preacher was likely to hold forth for at least an hour and to deliver as many as three sermons a week. He preached once or twice on Sundays and sometimes gave a week-day lecture or fast-day sermon. All of the activity took place in the context of Congregationalism.[18]

Unlike the Plymouth settlers, the Massachusetts Bay Puritans had to determine how their churches were to be organized. The immigrants had chafed under episcopal and royal control and had been obliged to work within the parish system, with its mixed congregations of the elect and the profane. They carried to the New World their vision of a truly reformed church. Among the factors that influenced them in their creation of what became the New England Way were five of special importance:

1. The congregational tendency of most of the clergymen who came. Many of the ministers shared the influence of William Ames and other proto-Congregationalists.

2. The desire for harmony if not uniformity among churches that functioned within a semi-sovereign commonwealth. Massachusetts Bay settlers from the beginning acted in a determinedly independent manner.

3. The willingness of ministers and influential laymen to accept as precedents the practices of the earliest churches. The Salem church, first in the Bay, served as a model for the founders of the Boston-Charlestown church, and the example was taken up rather generally. Having suitable models reduced anxiety that might otherwise have been overwhelming as men created a new culture in what they labelled a wilderness.

4. The intellectual leadership of Thomas Hooker and John Cotton. William Hubbard, writing in the 1680s, noted that the first arrivals were "by some sort of covenant soon moulded into a church in every plantation, where they took up their abode, until Mr. Cotton and Mr. Hooker came over, . . . who did clear up the order and method of church government according as they apprehended was most consonant to the word of God."

5. The felt need to justify their innovations to Puritans who remained in England. General agreement on principles was

necessary if the creators of New England Congregationalism were to defend themselves—as they were soon obliged to do—to the Protestant community of which they believed themselves to be a part.[19]

In an early statement, *The True Constitution of a Particular Visible Church, proved by Scripture* (composed 1634, published 1642), John Cotton notes that a church begins with Christians, those called to salvation by God. This is the "fellowship of the saints." The definitive statement of Congregationalism, the Cambridge Platform of 1648, describes a church as a body having a "visible political union" among members. By virtue of being a church, the members have had power given to them. "In respect of the body, or brotherhood of the church and power from Christ granted unto them," the government of the church "resembles a democracy." The members as a body have power to admit, admonish, and excommunicate members. The demands of Puritan moral theology were very severe, and those known to have sinned might well be required to make a public confession of guilt in order to maintain their membership. Admonition of a member prevented him from receiving the Lord's Supper until the church members were satisfied that his repentance was genuine.[20]

What this church fellowship consisted of is difficult to grasp. Something of its quality is shown by the records of the Boston church kept by Robert Keayne between November 1639 and May 1642. The bond between those who had joined the Boston church was so strong that even those who had deserted the church and left the colony were considered by those remaining to be their spiritual responsibility. Although admission may have been difficult, it was even more difficult for those who had been admitted to live free of the influence of the church. At least some of those admitted but later excommunicated so missed the sense of spiritual brotherhood and acceptance which came through membership that they found living without it very painful. Perhaps because church membership was so much valued by those admitted to it, few were excommunicated. During the years 1639 - 52, 652 adults were admitted to membership in the Boston church; seventeen people were publicly admonished, and only five were eventually excommunicated.[21]

How did a man enter into church fellowship? Traditionally, membership in a Christian church was open to everyone. Such was the practice in the England from which the New England Puritans had come. The practice worked out after the colonists arrived in

America was a novel one and became an important part of the New
England Way. A person who sought church membership was supposed to have evidence that he had been called to salvation. He had
to be a "visible saint." He was first questioned by the officers of the
church. John Cotton, writing about 1637, reported that these
questions were put to the candidates at his church.

How it pleased God to work in them to bring them home to Christ?
Whether the Law had convinced them of sin? How the Lord had won them
to deny themselves and their own righteousness and to rely on the
righteousness of Christ? Then they make a brief confession or else an
answer to a few questions about the main fundamental points of religion.

If the candidate was judged satisfactory, he was then proposed for
membership to the congregation, who were asked for testimony of
the candidate's "Christian and sincere affections." If he was com-
mended by the members, he might be asked to make a public confession, of perhaps fifteen minutes, of how he came to receive grace.
(In later years a public confession was a regular requirement, except
in Hooker's Hartford church and perhaps elsewhere in Connecticut.) Then if he was voted into membership he entered into covenant with God and the church. This was called "owning the
covenant." Candidates in Cotton's church were addressed as
follows:

Since it hath pleased God to move you, brethen, to hold forth the right
hand of fellowship, it is your part, and that which I am to require of you in
the name of the Lord and of his church before you can be admitted
thereunto, whether you be willing to enter a holy covenant with God and
with them and by the grace and help of Christ be willing to deny yourself
and all your former pollutions and corruptions, wherein in any sort you have
walked, and so to give yourself to the Lord Jesus, making him your only
priest and atonement, your only prophet, your only guide and king and
lawgiver, and to walk before him in all professed subjections unto all his
holy ordinance[s], according to the rule of the gospel, and to walk together
with his church and the members thereof in brotherly love and mutual
edification and succor according to God; then do I also promise unto you in
the name of this church that by the help of Christ we likewise will walk
towards you in all brotherly love and holy watchfulness to the mutual
building up one of another in the fellowship of the Lord Jesus Christ.
                                                        Amen, Amen.

Sometimes the conversion narratives of the candidates were recorded. Those that have survived follow the pattern of John

Winthrop's narrative, given above, and the sermons of Thomas Hooker. (See Chapter 4.) In admission to membership the details of dogma were not considered important. The vital considerations were a conversion experience and submission to the covenant.[22]

This procedure for admission to church membership was widely adopted in Massachusetts through the influence of John Cotton, who was the codifier of the New England Way and the religious leader of Boston. Its importance is great, among other reasons, because the church was at the heart of the community and because church membership was for many years a prerequisite to full citizenship in the commonwealth of Massachusetts Bay. Cotton wrote two full statements: *The Way of the Churches of Christ in New-England* (London, 1645), a description of Congregational practice in New England, and *The Keyes of the Kingdom of Heaven* (London, 1644), a description of the power and authority of the church. The former is much more interesting than the latter, a polemic addressed to the Westminster Assembly in England, which was attempting to form a new policy for the Church of England. Later Cotton wrote two other ecclesiastical works, *The Way of the Congregational Churches Cleared* (London, 1648), and *Of the Holiness of Church Members* (London, 1650). Other New England divines contributed books also, notably John Norton and Richard Mather. An official statement was in time adopted, the aforementioned Cambridge Platform.[23]

The heart of the New England Way, and the most obviously unique feature of New England Puritanism, was the church covenant. The Puritans found the covenant all through the Old Testament. Abraham's family had entered into a "church estate" by a covenant with Abraham; the "church in the wilderness" led by Moses was a church formed by covenant. "It is evident," declared John Cotton, "by the light of nature that all civil relations are founded in covenant." There is no other way, he believed, by which a people can freely unite together. John Winthrop explains, "Leave out the covenant and let us see what manner of churches you will constitute. Suppose ten or twenty Christians were desirous to constitute a church. These being met together, every one of them makes a confession of his faith. Will this make them a church? I conceive it will pass the skill of a good logician to make a church without some contract or agreement such as will amount to a covenant."[24]

When newcomers arrived in Massachusetts, Cotton explained, they could either join an established church or if a number came at the same time and wished to remain together, they might establish a new church. They were expected to profess that "it was the principal end of their coming to enjoy the presence of the Lord in the liberty and purity of his ordinances." To gather a new church, the new arrivals first located a gifted man to guide them, usually one who had been a preacher in England and one that they would later ask to take office among them. They then met for prayer and conference until they were satisfied of one another's spiritual estate, and then they made plans to enter church fellowship on a given day. They invited officers and brethren from nearby churches and, in Massachusetts, the magistrates also, since they are "nursing fathers to the church." (Approval by the General Court, the colony's legislative body, was required for the gathering of a new church.)[25]

The original covenant of one of the first churches of the colony, the Boston-Charlestown church, is as follows:

In the name of our Lord Jesus Christ and in obedience to his holy will and divine ordinance: We whose names are hereunder written, being by his most wise and good providence brought together into this part of America in the Bay of Massachusetts, and desirous to unite ourselves into one congregation or church under the Lord Jesus Christ as our head, in such sort as becometh all those whom he hath redeemed and sanctified to himself, do hereby solemnly and religiously (as in his most holy presence) promise and bind ourselves to walk in all our ways according to the rule of the gospel and in all sincere conformity to his holy ordinances and in mutual love and respect each to other, so near as God shall give us grace.[26]

The size of a church was to be determined by how many could comfortably hear the preaching of the Word and receive the sacrament of the Lord's Supper. Only members could receive it. Most towns had only one church, which met at the meeting house, also used for town meetings. The congregational form of church government encouraged the development of democracy in the civil government of the town. Town meeting and church meeting were in many ways analogous. Boston, which became the largest town, did not have a second church until 1650, when the North Church was founded. The insistence on a conversion experience as a requisite for admission to membership meant that numbers of people were not members—apparently they simply did not apply, since few who did apply were rejected—and since only church members had the franchise, large numbers of people were not participating members of the commonwealth, though they might have a voice in local affairs. The law was that "no man shall be admitted to the freedom of this body politic but such as are members of some of the churches within the limits of the same."[27]

III *Church and State*

The polity of the churches was worked out on the soil of New England. What of the state? The political leaders of Massachusetts Bay, under the governorship of John Winthrop, interpreted their charter as a grant of semi-sovereign status. They referred to their political society not as a colony but as a commonwealth, and the government and laws they created for it were a reflection of the authority that they judged to be theirs, for the political, social, and legal structures that they devised were remarkably different from what they had known in the Old World. While there were some disagreements over the distribution of power, the leaders and at least the heads of most households agreed that the basis for the new society was to be devotion to godliness. This attitude is reflected in a letter from a layman, James Cudworth, written to an English friend in 1634: "And with all such as you shall advise to sit down with us, we should entreat you that they may be such as you judge to be fit to be received into church fellowship."[28]

The relation that developed between church and state in Puritan Massachusetts was close, though the two were separate. The Cambridge Platform declared that the "power and authority of magistrates" is "for helping and furthering" the churches: "It is part of that honor due to Christian magistrates to desire and crave the consent and approbation" of the churches which provide "encouragement and comfort. . . . The end of the magistrate's office is not only the quiet and peaceable life of the subject in matters of righteousness and honesty but also in matters of godliness, yea, of all godliness." And the preface to *The Book of the General Lawes and Libertyes of Massachusetts Bay* observed that in New England "our churches and civil state have been planted and grown up (like two twins) together like that of Israel" in such a fashion that "each do help and strengthen [the] other, the churches, the civil authority and the civil authority, the churches."[29]

John Cotton explained that "God's institutions (such as the government of church and of commonwealth) may be close and compact, and co-ordinate one to another, and yet not confounded.

God hath so framed the state of church government and ordinances that they may be compatible to any commonwealth, though never so much disordered in his frame. But yet when a commonwealth hath liberty to mold his own frame (*scripturae plentitudinem adoro*), I conceive the scripture hath given full direction for the right ordering of the same and that in such sort as may best maintain the *euexia* [vigor] of the church." The Scriptures, Puritan leaders explained, taught that political power is best restricted to godly men, "fit material for church fellowship." It would be dangerous to give to ungodly men the power, which freemen enjoy, of electing magistrates and representatives to the Court, since only with godly men in control would commonwealth and church be safe. Thomas Shepard, preaching an election sermon to the General Court in 1638, was more emphatic. "Maintain the privilege to death," he told the electors. "Whomsoever you shall choose, let him be one from among yourselves, a member of some church. He that is shut out of the fellowship of the churches will be an enemy unto the strictness of churches, and ruin churches, you ruin state."[30]

The cooperation between the churches and the commonwealth of Massachusetts Bay that was developed came to flourish because both church and state were founded on the idea of covenant. It was the central instrument by which men could live harmoniously together. Though the relationship sometimes created problems, both ministers and magistrates considered the connection to be absolutely indispensable. Only when Massachusetts lost its charter in 1684 and thus its independence was the relationship disrupted. John Winthrop wrote that "It is of the nature and essence of every society to be knit together by some covenant, either expressed or implied." On this concept rested one of Winthrop's first acts as governor in 1630: the extension of the franchise to all of the colony's males, except servants. Under the charter issued by King Charles's government the people had no political rights, and though later the franchise was limited to church members, Winthrop seems to have believed that the extension was an act of covenanting. Thus he wrote in 1637: "The essential form of a commonweal or body politic such as this is, ... I take to be this—the consent of a certain company of people to cohabit together under one government for their mutual safety and welfare." He went on to reach these conclusions:

1. No commonweal can be founded but by free consent.
2. The persons so incorporating have a public and relative interest each

in other, and in the place of their cohabitation and goods and laws, etc., and in all the means of their welfare so as none can claim privilege with them but by free consent.

3. The nature of such an incorporation ties every member thereof to seek out and entertain all means that may conduce to the welfare of the body and to keep off whatsoever doth appear to tend to their damage.

4. The welfare of the whole is not to be put to apparent hazard for the advantage of any particular members.

Though Winthrop and others cited the covenant principle of voluntary association for the creation of a political body, Puritans did not explore the origins of society or the rights of man in a state of nature, as Hobbes and Locke were to do.[31]

IV   *High Hopes and Disappointments*

The fact that in the late 1630s and 1640s the church covenant included only a fraction of the population while the social covenant included all of the inhabitants of the commonwealth might have been more disconcerting had it not been for the conviction of many of the religious leaders that the discrepancy was not likely to be a continuing one. When they came to America committed Puritans expected that many of the unconverted with them would be called to salvation. For a while their hopes seemed to be well grounded. John Cotton reported that "sundry elder and younger persons who came hither not out of respect to conscience or spiritual ends but out of respect to friends or outward enlargement [prosperity] have here found that grace which they sought not for." Cotton was only one of many who believed that the creation of pure churches in America was a clear indication that the millennium would soon occur, and it would be preceded, they thought, by such an outpouring of God's spirit that saving grace would be given to large numbers of the unregenerate.[32]

Intense Puritan piety was often accompanied by a strong wish that Christ would come again to rule the earth, as the Puritans believed the books of Daniel and Revelation had prophesied. Many Protestant Biblical commentators were convinced that the world was coming to an end in the seventeenth century, with divine judgments on Roman Catholicism, which they labelled Antichrist. In the 1620s and 1630s the limitations placed on godly preachers and the tense political situation gave English Puritans a sense of active participation in a cosmic struggle.[33]

This excitement carried some Puritans across the sea to New England, where the establishment of pure churches was considered a sign that the millennium had almost arrived. Thomas Tillam expressed his joy "Upon the first sight of New England, June 29, 1638," in a poem, to which he provided scriptural verses as a marginal gloss: "And everyone that hath forsaken houses, or brethren, or sisters, or father, or mother, or wife, or children, or lands, for my name's sake, shall receive an hundredfold, and shall inherit everlasting life" (Matthew 29:1). "Then shall the king say unto them on his right hand, Come, ye blessed of my Father, inherit the kingdom prepared for you from the foundation of the world" (Matthew 25:34). Here is Tillam's excited verse:

> Hail, holy land wherein our holy lord
> Hath planted his most true and holy word.
> Hail, happy people who have disposed
> Yourself of friends and means to find some rest
> For your poor wearied souls, oppressed of late
> For Jesus' sake, with envy, spite, and hate.
> To you that blessed promise truly's given
> Of sure reward, which you'll receive in heaven.
> Methinks I hear the Lamb of God thus speak:
> Come, my dear little flock, who for my sake
> Have left your country, dearest friends, and goods
> And hazarded your lives o' th' raging floods;
> Possess this country, free from all annoy.
> Here I'll be with you; here you shall enjoy
> My sabbaths, sacraments, my ministry,
> And ordinances in their purity.
>
> Prepare to hear your sentence thus expressed:
> Come ye, my servants of my Father blessed.[34]

In the years 1639 - 41 John Cotton preached a whole series of sermons on chapters of Revelation. He foresaw 1655 to be the year when God would act. Many other New England preachers taught similarly. The fullest statement of the millennial expectations is that expressed by Edward Johnson in his extravagant *History of New-England,* published in 1654; it is best known by its running title, *Wonder-working Providence of Zion's Saviour in America.* Johnson saw the whole history and development as ordained by God. He proclaims, with conviction, "The winter is passed, the rain is changed and gone; come out of the holes of the secret places. Fear not because your number is but small; gather into churches, and let Christ be your king."[35]

Johnson asks if the creation of New England is not to be seen as the beginning of Christ's reign on earth:

Then judge all you whom the Lord Christ hath given a discerning spirit, whether these poor New England people be not the forerunners of Christ's army, and the marvelous providences which you shall now hear be not the very finger of God, and whether the Lord hath not sent this people to preach in this wilderness, and to proclaim to all nations the near approach of the most wonderful works that ever the sons of men saw. Will not you believe that a nation can be born in a day? Here is a work come very near it, but if you will believe you shall see far greater things than these, and that in a very little time. . . .

Another who believed that the millennium had actually arrived in New England noted, "Is not the government in church and commonweal (according to God's own rules) that new heaven and earth promised, and the first fruits begun in this poor New England?"[36]

When the English revolution began, several New England leaders returned to England to participate in the efforts there to create a new Kingdom of God on earth. The dreams of New England Puritans slowly died in disappointment when the New England Way was not adopted as a model by the English, whose revolution ultimately failed.[37]

New England Puritans were left with churches that had to cope with large numbers of nonmembers. John Winthrop's hope expressed in 1630 that "We must be knit together in this work [of constructing a holy commonwealth] as one man" was scarcely realized in the years after 1640. Ministers were indeed considered town officials and were paid from town revenue; attendance at church was required of all, both members and nonmembers, though by Puritan doctrine only the children of church members could be baptized. But in Boston in 1645 of the 421 families living there, 128 had neither husband nor wife as a church member. As time went on, the percentage of the population that belonged to the church grew even smaller.[38]

Eventually the decrease in church membership was to trouble New England sorely. The nature of the conflict within the New England churches is suggested by Ernest Troeltsch's classic analysis of the types of ecclesiastical organizations. Troeltsch distinguished between what he called church-types and sect-types: "The Church is that type of organization which is overwhelmingly conservative, which to a certain extent accepts the secular order and dominates the masses; in principle, therefore, it is universal, i.e., it desires to cover the whole life of humanity." This description quite nicely fits the churches of early Puritan Massachusetts, where church and state operated harmoniously and where all the civil leaders were church members who sought guidance on many issues from the ministers. But Troeltsch's definition of the sect-type is also applicable to the Puritan churches. The sects, he wrote, "are comparatively small groups; they aspire after personal inward perfection, and they aim at a direct personal fellowship between the members of each group." This is an apt description of the Puritan ecclesiastical ideal. But, as Troeltsch also observes, such sects "are forced to organize in small groups and to renounce the idea of dominating the world." The Puritans insisted that church membership be restricted to the elect, but they sought to dominate the entire population, the whole of life and society, to create a theocracy in which both civil and church leaders, working together, did God's will. The theological and ecclesiastical principles of New England Puritanism were full of such tensions, ambiguities, paradoxes.[39]

V *Covenant Theology*

The concepts of the social covenant and the church covenant flourished in American Puritanism because they reinforced each other, and because both were reinforced by covenant theology. The latter was derived from law and government, with their notions of allegiance, contracts, alliances. It originated in the free cities of Germany and in Swiss cantons where Protestants needed to appeal to the franchised class. Four fundamental aspects of the covenant idea in theology can be noted. First, the covenant implies some sort of agreement between God and man with mutual obligations. In Calvin's words, it is "as if God had said, 'See how kindly I indulge thee, . . . for whereas I owe thee nothing, I condescend graciously to engage in a mutual covenant.' " Second, man's obligation is to do what God would have him to do. Again, Calvin explains, "In all covenants of his mercy, the Lord requires of his servants in return uprightness and sanctity of life." Third, the covenant between God and man originated in Old Testament times and continues through history. Calvin writes, "The covenant made with the patriarchs is so much like ours in substance and reality that the two are actually one

and the same. Yet they differ in mode of operation." Among the
differences that Calvin mentions are that in Old Testament times
God emphasized earthly benefits; in New Testament times he
reveals "the grace of the future life," and that the Old Testament
dealt with types and figures, "shadow in place of the substance";
the New Testament reveals "the very substance of truth." Fourth,
the covenant is a covenant of grace that succeeds an earlier covenant, the covenant of works. This idea, developed after Calvin, is
set forth in the theology of the English Puritan Dudley Fenner, and
after him by William Perkins.[40]

In England, covenant theology was adopted by the Puritans and
was employed by Cartwright, Perkins, and Ames, among others.
Most Massachusetts ministers of the first generation taught its principles, and several American Puritans wrote works of covenant
theology: Thomas Hooker's *The Covenant of Grace Opened* (1649)
and John Cotton's *A Treatise of the Covenant of Grace* (1659) are
examples. The most elaborate treatment is Peter Bulkeley's *The
Gospel Covenant* (1646; second edition, 1651). Covenant theology
was chiefly used, to begin with, because it lent itself to an
evangelical approach: it made the conversion process as understandable as a business transaction, and it made redemption rest on
mutuality. Later Puritans developed its implications into a kind of
voluntarism, to the neglect of the Calvinist doctrines of irresistible
grace. Michael McGiffert has recently emphasized the importance
and function of covenant theology, especially as set forth by Peter
Bulkeley: "More than a formal tenet, the covenant also exerted
great affective force; charged with evangelical, even millennial passion, not only did it articulate the inured experience of grace, and so
tapped the deepest springs of piety, but it also lent itself to an ex-
traordinary set of social uses." Bulkeley recognized, notes
McGiffert, that it was "an instrument of collective identity, purpose, and order."[41]

Like others, Peter Bulkeley, first minister of Concord,
Massachusetts, asserts the existence of three covenants. The first is
the covenant between the Father and the Son, by which the Son
agrees to perform the functions of redeemer and mediator on the
condition that he and his followers will be given glory. The second,
the breaking of which made the covenant of redemption necessary,
is the covenant of works. It is applicable to Adam and beyond Adam
to all men—unless they can get out from under its terms and get
within the third, the covenant of grace. The covenant of works and

the covenant of grace have much in common. Both were authored by God; both involve two parties, God and man; both are intended for the manifestation of God's glory; both promise life and blessedness; both require a condition for attaining what they promise.

But the two also differ. The covenant of works was made with man in his integrity, when he was able to keep its terms: it requires the leading of a perfectly righteous life on the basis of man's own ability. Just one transgression of God's law, which is known in the first place by the light of nature, means that the covenant is broken and man is damned. This covenant, intended to reveal God's justice, cannot possibly be kept by any man since Adam's fall, by which all men were corrupted. The covenant of works continues in effect through all time. It was renewed at Mount Sinai in the giving of the law to Moses.

Although this covenant of works cannot be kept by any man, it performs important functions besides revealing God's justice. It prepares man for Christ and the covenant of grace by revealing how inadequate man is to save himself, and it shows how men who have entered the covenant of grace should try to live. The covenant of grace was first preached after the Fall in Genesis 3:15, when God told the serpent that the seed of woman would bruise its head. Later it was delivered to Abraham when God promised that the Messiah would come of his seed and that he and all that believe in that seed should be blessed. This covenant, from Adam to the end of the world, remains the same. But Bulkeley explains, as Calvin had, that there are two modes of dispensation of the covenant of grace: the old covenant of grace in Old Testament times and the new covenant of grace in New Testament times and later. The seals of the old covenant are circumcision and the passover; in new covenant times the seals are baptism and the Lord's Supper. In old covenant times prescribed ceremonies provided "types and figures of spiritual things," later fully revealed under the new covenant. (On typology, see Chapter 4.). Thus in Old Testament times blood sacrifice "typed out" Christ's death on the cross. Thus Moses, acting as a mediator between God and the Israelites, typed out Christ's role as mediator. Thus the promises of a better land, Canaan, typed out the promises of a better land, heaven.

Just as the covenant of works had made promises upon a condition, so does the covenant of grace, which requires faith in the promises of the covenant. The great promise is "I will be your God and you shall be my people." If man accepts God as his God, then God accepts man as His own and will provide him with spiritual and temporal blessings. Being God's man, however, requires living according to a prescribed way of life, God's way. Such righteous living is possible only through grace, the only cause of man's salvation. From God's point of view the covenant scheme has three steps. First, God prescribes a way of life to man, a way that is also the road to salvation. Second, God then "brings us first through the door of faith." He then "carries us to the end of our faith, the salvation of our souls." Or, to put it another way, "The Lord comes and takes away the heart of stone, that evil heart of unbelief, and gives us a spirit of faith and renewing grace, and then draweth the soul into a covenant with him to walk with him in a way of faith, depending upon him by faith, and obeying him by faith." The covenant is conditional, but God provides the condition.[42]

Since Bulkeley's *Gospel Covenant* is a collection of sermons, his aim is to speak to the condition of his hearers, his Concord congregation in the 1640s. To those not within the covenant, he provides directions on how to get within it. To those that are doubtful, he provides hope that they are already within it. To those who believe themselves within it, he explains how to make sure that they are and what the responsibilities are to those within. He labors at length the thesis that sanctification is a sign of justification; that is, that those within have assurance of salvation through the good works they are able to perform. (On the debate over sanctification, see Chapter 3.) Bulkeley emphasizes in detail the distinctions between the covenant of grace and the covenant of works and insists that trying to be saved by the covenant of works is different from following the Law when one is under the covenant of grace. But he also insists that the covenant of grace requires "holiness in all those that claim any part in it." He writes, "Let such as are pure and undefiled in their way, let them rejoice in their portion; all the blessings of the covenant are theirs; God is yours, life is yours, heaven is yours." Thus Bulkeley comes perilously close to the greatest danger that covenant theology creates: failing to maintain the distinction between works and grace. When Bulkeley exhorts men to "express their holiness in their lives and ways that they may thereby approve themselves to be faithful in their covenant with God," he is at least very close to ignoring the distinction.[43]

The impulse towards voluntarism, towards demanding that men assume responsibility for their own eternal fate, developed in Massachusetts as the ministers discovered that despite their best preaching efforts, many of their hearers remained unconverted. The tendency grew in strength, as we shall see, in opposition to Anne Hutchinson and her followers, who combined with their insistence that works are no test of salvation, the doctrine that in conversion the soul is wholly passive.

At times, in his efforts to appeal to the unconverted, Bulkeley comes close to the Arminian doctrine, condemned by the Synod of Dort, that grace is resistible. Thus he declares:

. . . there is danger in sinning against the covenant of works, but it is more dangerous to sin against grace. For there is help for such as break the covenant of works, but no help for such as make void the covenant of grace to themselves. These are the killing and destroying sins that leave no remedy. It is true (as was said before) that the Lord passeth by many weaknesses of his servants that desire and endeavor to cleanse themselves from all filthiness and spareth them as a father his son (Malachi 3:17). But contemptuous sins against grace are beyond all help. This is to sin desperately. Herein men stumble at the stumbling stone. They think that now under the days of grace (though they be yet under the Law) they may sin without danger and continue in their evils, but here the danger is greatest; therefore take heed how you make grace your enemy. If the Law condemns us, grace may save us. But if grace save us not, who shall plead for us?

How do men "make the covenant of grace void unto themselves"? asks Bulkeley. "By neglecting and slighting the offers and tenders of grace which are made unto them." Bulkeley seeks to persuade men to accept the offers that he believes God is making through him as preacher. But orthodox reformed theology holds that these offers are not themselves grace, though grace may accompany them. As the Westminster Confession puts it, the elect are effectively called by God's "Word and Spirit." Though the grace of faith "is ordinarily wrought by the ministry of the Word," it is accompanied by "the work of the spirit in their hearts."[44]

VI *Moralism*

New England Puritanism is rightly famous for its high moral standards, enforced by both church and state. Each church member was expected to watch over every other. Those who were not members were likewise the proper concern of Christians, for, as

Thomas Hooker taught, "A man's corruption may be restrained and kept in from any actual breaking out, not for any good that he in himself shall reap thereby but for others' benefit, for the good of society in general, the good of some in special." Hooker himself kept careful watch, and when he saw some kind of sin breaking out, he would "take a text on purpose, wherein it is plainly condemned." Hooker taught that nonmembers and members should see that their sins prevent salvation: ". . . if you will have sin dwell in your soul, God will never dwell with you, nor shall you ever dwell with him." Again, ". . . either I must lose my sin or my soul, there is no other thing to be done."[45]

After Thomas Hooker left Massachusetts for Connecticut, and John Cotton found his reputation somewhat tarnished, as we shall see, by the Anne Hutchinson affair, Thomas Shepard of Cambridge was considered a guardian of order and orthodoxy. Like Bulkeley, Shepard tended to blur the distinction between the two covenants in such a way as to promote a reliance on works. He taught that one who has entered the covenant of grace should recognize that "in respect of his natural being in himself," he is still under the Law and will remain under it permanently. The saint must distinguish between "himself as he is in Christ" and "himself as he is growing on his first root," which is thoroughly corrupt. Whenever a saint sins, he must cultivate "legal humility" by which he acknowledges in his heart that he "deserves death" after even a small and involuntary offense. Involuntary sins are, according to Shepard, worse than voluntary ones, just as the man who is by nature a thief is worse than the man who chooses deliberately to be a thief.[46]

Shepard has much to say about the bondage of natural men to their own lusts and to the power of Satan. He contrasts this bondage to the saints' liberty, which consists of receiving Christ as one's prince and submitting oneself wholly to him. Shepard urges man to bring his every thought "into subjection and obedience to Christ." Being able to do so is a means of distinguishing oneself from a hypocrite, one who has joined a church though he has not been called to salvation. Shepard admits that "if hypocrites could be openly and ecclesiastically discerned, they should not be received in, nor kept in, because matter fit to ruin a church are not fit to make a church." Therefore men must be their brothers' keepers; they must avoid excessive charity and "bear a jealous heart." Just as one should judge one's fellows severely, so should one judge oneself severely. It is not enough to look for grace from God, for one may

do so much and still be an "evangelical hypocrite." The faith that
Shepard would have man possess is one that creates in the believer a
continuing necessity to seek assurance of salvation in his good
works. By constantly doing them and noting his ability to do them,
one can avoid the threat of damnation that Shepard seeks to keep
always before men. Thus Shepard encourages not piety but a stern
moralism, not faith but works.[47]

VII　*The Covenant and Baptism*

Historically, one of the most influential aspects of covenant
theology is its teaching on children. Bulkeley teaches that just as
God's old covenant with Abraham was also with his seed, so under
the new, when one enters the covenant his children do also "to a
thousand generations." Thus if one's parents are within the covenant, he may "go to God and plead the covenant" of his father and
hope to receive grace. Because of this relationship, the Cambridge
Platform declares, the term *saints* includes church members and
"the children of such, who are also holy." Thomas Hooker is more
explicit than Bulkeley on the status of the "children of the
covenant." He contends that God may use those within the covenant as a means of salvation to their children because "believing
parents when they enter into a visible covenant to walk in God's
ways, they enter not for themselves alone but for all that come of
them; and God doth engage himself by these means to work grace
in their hearts"—and Hooker adds, cautiously, "as He sees fit." The
children automatically receive grace when their parents are under
the covenant, but such grace, "federal grace," is not saving grace
and may be lost. ("Federal" is derived from the Latin for covenant,
foederus.)[48]

According to Hooker, the child of a saint is "made partaker of the
covenant with the father, and by the father God hath promised that
[the father's taking hold of the covenant] should be a means; not
that the father conveys grace to the child (that is a dream) but He
uses the father as a means and will communicate to the child as He
sees fit. . . ." Because God is likely to use the parents as a means of
grace, the children of those in the covenant probably will be saved
and therefore may be baptized, just as the children of those within
the old covenant of grace were circumcised. For the Puritans, baptism and the Lord's Supper are "seals of election," seals of the covenant of grace. "The seals," said Hooker, "do not give the first grace
but do presuppose that such as do receive them are within the covenant of grace."[49]

Eventually, baptism was to become a much disputed issue, one that took years to resolve. Baptism was to be followed, Hooker and other preachers assumed, by conversion, when the baptized child reached adulthood. In America, they assumed, with preachers free from the restrictions placed on them by the bishops, saving grace would flow freely. Some who anticipated that the millenium was coming knew that a great outflowing of grace was to precede it. Winthrop recorded in his journal that in the 1630s "Divers profane and notorious evil persons came and confessed their sins and were comfortably received into the bosom of the church." But ten years later enthusiasm had waned. What, wondered some Puritans, had their baptism meant? Those who had travelled miles in old England to hear a godly preacher found that he was much less exciting when heard week after week.[50]

VIII   *The Native Americans*

While the Massachusetts Bay colony had been still in the planning stage, its leaders agreed that one of the most important motives for migration was conversion of the Indians. The Puritans were not, however, seriously interested in Indian missions except for propaganda purposes, and they made high demands of anyone who would be converted. He had to know the Bible well, and an Algonquian version of the Bible was not published until John Eliot brought one out in 1663. In the meanwhile, few ministers were willing to invest the time needed to learn the Indians' language. Moreover, the Puritans made a conversion to white man's ways a prerequisite for religious conversion. An important consideration was Congregational church policy. Without a central administration, no clergymen were available except ministers tied to a congregation, since the church members, the saints, selected the minister and paid him to serve them. John Eliot, the most famous missionary, remained minister of the Roxbury church; to his missionary work he gave only one day every other week. In time, there were some successes, but these occurred only after 1650, twenty years after the colony was created.[51]

IX   *Puritan Paradoxes*

The major Puritan concerns during the first years of the Massachusetts Bay colony were the teaching of orthodox Puritanism, the establishment of Congregationalism, the founding of pure churches, and the creation of a strong social order based on the covenant. All were closely related. More significantly, all were riddled with inner conflicts. Puritan doctrine was, to begin with, evangelical: the central point of the Puritan's life was supposed to be conversion, but having once received saving grace, one was expected to submit oneself constantly to self-examination to make certain that one was really saved. Covenant theology was supposed to lend itself to effective evangelism, but before long it made conversion seem more difficult, since it taught that God's grace was most likely to be enjoyed only after a long and difficult process of preparation. The church and the commonwealth were to walk together harmoniously so that all of society and life were devoted to God's glory. But the Puritan concern with church discipline, with the exclusion of hypocrites from the church, and with the limitation of the franchise to church members inevitably created a society wherein the saints were powerful and the unchurched were less than second-class citizens.

The seeds of Puritan decay have been located in the growth of commercialism, the fragmentation of society through population growth and new settlements, an increase in individualism in a capitalistic society, and an increasingly unequal distribution of wealth. But the paradoxical nature of American Puritanism itself is at least as important as these external forces. The decline was hastened by polarization, with which Roger Williams and Anne Hutchinson, two troublers of the new Israel, had much to do.

CHAPTER 3

The Crystallization of Puritanism

T HE work of the founders of New England Puritanism was not undertaken in a vacuum. While there was remarkable agreement among the leaders on theological and ecclesiastical issues, there were disputes from as early as 1631 when Winthrop was obliged to visit Watertown to attempt to resolve a dispute that was dividing the church. Soon broader and more fundamental issues came into focus. The earliest opposition leaders were not unsympathetic with Puritan ideals; indeed, they had come to New England because of them. But Puritans in England had been united chiefly in opposition to the bishops and their demands. In New England, with Puritans in control of a semi-independent state, leaders believed that harmony and agreement were necessary for survival, and those who could not or would not embrace the practical but paradoxical Puritanism that was being established in Massachusetts were considered divisive forces. If they had not been so outspoken, or if they had been less popular or powerful, they might have been tolerated. Instead, their efforts to create change resulted in the polarization and codification of increasingly legalistic Puritan policies and doctrine. Analysis of their attacks on orthodox New England Puritanism reveals the assumptions on which the Puritan commonwealth rested.

I Roger Williams

The most extended critique of the new commonwealth, one that extended over fifteen years, was made by a clergyman, Roger Williams. He was only twenty-seven when he arrived in Massachusetts in 1631; his wife was only wenty-one. Most of the other ministers were much older. If Williams could not offer the wide experience that Cotton and Hooker had, he was undeniably a man of charm and character, and the Boston church, needing a minister since John Wilson was to return to England to get his wife, elected him to be their teacher. But he refused to join the church because, as Winthrop put it, "they would not make a public declaration of their repentance for having communion with the churches of England while they lived there, and besides, had declared his opinion that the magistrate [the civil authority] might not punish the breach of the Sabbath nor any other offence as it was a breach of the first table," that is, the first four of the Ten Commandments. Williams was a Separatist and, moreover, a believer in the absolute separation of church and state.[1]

He was willing, however, to accept a position with the Salem church, where he soon became very popular. He nevertheless moved shortly afterwards to Separatist Plymouth, where he served for less than a year before returning to Salem. During the next two and a half years he questioned many of the fundamental positions of Massachusetts before choosing to head for Rhode Island rather than be deported to England. Later, in the 1640s, he again attacked the foundations of Bay policy, this time in writing.[2]

Having arrived in the New World less than a year after the Winthrop Fleet in 1630, Williams must have been struck by the changes that Puritanism had undergone as a result of the freedom from control by English authority. A visitor who arrived in 1635 commented that "God's people are come into a new country where they freely enjoy the liberty of his holy ordinances without any trouble or molestation at all, either of bishop, archbishop, or any other inferior carping minister or gaping officer, so they come unto the land and the Lord with new hearts and new lives. . . ." Williams seems to have supposed that the process of renewal and purification was to be a continuing one. He saw, for instance, that the "matter and form of a church" was not known "among God's people themselves (till yesterday)," and he celebrated what he called "that gallant and heavenly and fundamental principle" that church members should be "actual believers." This was a truth he himself had discovered by "search and examination and considerations" and by these means he could discover, he thought, new truths.[3]

For Williams, perhaps the deepest truth was the absolute opposition between Jesus Christ and the world. Williams contrasted "the purity of Christ" with "the world upon whom the vials and plagues and vengeance are to be poured." Because this was his world view, Williams objected to any practice or even any terminology that blurred the distinction between the world and Christ. Thus he strenuously attacked the use of the word *Christendom* since the great bulk of its inhabitants were not Christians. In Massachusetts the separation between Christians and the world was not nearly so absolute as Williams believed it should be. In the new commonwealth all residents of a town, church members and non-members alike, were expected to attend services together, though only members could receive the Lord's Supper. Williams maintained that the distinction was not carried far enough, since other aspects of God's worship were contaminated by the presence of the unregenerate. They should not be permitted to attend church services. He argued that Christians enjoyed full communion not only through the sacrament but also through sharing sermons, prayer, and each other's fellowship. Preaching to the converted is feeding Christ's flock. For the unconverted even to hear such preaching was to mix "the unclean and clean, of the flock of Christ and herds of the world together." Since all ordinances of the church are, according to Williams, of the same nature, requiring nonmembers to hear sermons is as bad as requiring them to receive the Lord's Supper. Williams insisted on the purity of God's worship to the extent that (according to Winthrop's report) he taught that a Christian should not even pray with the unconverted, even if it meant excluding one's own wife or child.[4]

Williams's most systematic attack on Massachusetts Bay Puritanism was made in the course of his debate with John Cotton. Six separate publications appeared in the process of the argument, of which the most important are Williams's *The Bloudy Tenent of Persecution* (1644) and Cotton's reply, *The Bloudy Tenent, Washed and Made White in the Bloud of the Lambe* (1647). In the debate Cotton's role was that of spokesman for the standing order; Williams was a severe critic of that order—one who admired it so much that he was the more disappointed to find the new commonwealth not all that it should be. The root of the difference was the relationship of church and state. In Massachusetts the separation between the two was far greater than in England; for example, no civil punishments, such as fines, could be administered by the church. In fact, in Massachusetts there was no church that the state could establish or give authority to; there were only separate congregations whose ministers were not institutionally related. But the civil government did supervise the formation of new churches and could summon ministers to synods (though the Cambridge Platform notes that the "constituting" of a synod is an ecclesiastical, not a civil act), and the state compelled nonmembers to attend religious services and to support the minister as well as limited the franchise to church members. [5]

The political-religious model for the Massachusetts commonwealth was Israel. Like the Hebrews, the Puritans were, as John Cotton saw it, in covenant with God. His laws were applicable to Massachusetts as to Israel, "because God, who was then bound up in covenant with them [the Hebrews] to be their God, hath put us in their stead and is become our God as well as theirs and hence we are as much bound to their laws as well as themselves." The Puritan view of the relationship of church and state can be described as organic. Cotton puts it this way:

If it was a part of the misery of the Gentiles to be aliens from the commonwealth of Israel (Ephesians 2:12), then 'tis a part of the happiness of Christian nations that they are subject to the laws of the commonwealth of Israel, and to be strangers from the commonwealth of Israel is not to be a church, because that is to be strangers from the promise, that is, from the covenant of the church and so from the civil covenant. Christ is king of church and commonwealth. So far as it [the church] varies from the commonwealth of Israel, so far is Christ from being king of the church. So far as the commonwealth varies from the laws of the church, so far is Christ from being king of the commonwealth. Christ is head of all principalities and powers for the church, and he will subordinate all kingdoms one day to the church.

In the Bloudy Tenent, Washed Cotton declares that "Christ never abolished a national civil state" such as Israel was; on the contrary "Christ hath enjoined (even as mediator) an everlasting kingdom not only in the church but in the government of all the kingdoms of the earth. . . ." [6]

The Puritans could identify Massachusetts with Israel because, as explained above, they saw the covenant of grace to be fundamentally the same before and after Christ's coming. But Williams found a radical difference between Jews and Christians, between "a follower of Moses" and a follower of Jesus Christ. The Old Testament had foreshadowed the New, but the way of the New is wholly spiritual. The kingdom of Christ is not an earthly kingdom nor a civil commonwealth. It is the spiritual kingdom of the church, and whereas "God gave unto that national church of the Jews that excellent land of Canaan and therein houses furnished, orchards, gardens, vineyards, olive yards, fields, wells, etc.,. . . God's people are now in the Gospel brought into a spiritual land of Canaan, flowing with spiritual milk and honey, and they abound with spiritual and heavenly comforts, though in a poor and persecuted condition." The world of nature remains totally corrupted, even its purest churches. "The world lies in wickedness, is like a wilderness or a sea of wild beasts innumerable, fornicators, covetous, idolaters, etc."[7]

According to Cotton and other spokesmen for Massachusetts Puritanism, theocracy is "the best form of government in the commonwealth as well as in the church." The functions of church and state differ and their powers are distinct, but both state and church should seek to serve God. The concern of the state is chiefly with men's bodies but secondarily with their souls. Though the people call the magistrates to their office, they have, Winthrop declared, "authority from God." According to Williams, however, the power of the magistrate derives not from God but only from the people, and therefore he can exercise no authority over spiritual matters, which belong to God, not to men. "It is but flattering of magistrates," wrote Williams; "it is but the accursed trusting to an arm of flesh to persuade the rulers of the earth that they are kings of Israel or church of God, who were in their institutions and government immediately from God, the rulers and governors of his holy church and people."[8]

Williams urged an absolute separation of church and state. The concern of the state should be solely men's bodies and their worldly goods. For this end the government should prescribe behavior but it has no concern with men's souls or with God's worship. Nor should only church members act as civil rulers, according to Williams, who did not believe that God restricted leadership ability to church members. Failure to recognize talents wherever they may be found means that they "must all lie buried in the earth." For Williams there is no such thing as a "Christian captain, Christian merchant, physician, lawyer, pilot, father, master, and (so consequently) magistrate."[9]

Puritans such as Winthrop and Cotton saw the creation of the new Israel as a climactic event in human history. Williams considered *all* Christians to be members of the new, spiritual Israel. But he wrote that "Nature knows no difference between [men] . . . in blood, birth, bodies." He judged that the special place that Cotton claimed for Massachusetts Bay was "to pull God and Christ and Spirit out of Heaven and subject them unto material, sinful, inconstant men. . . ."[10]

As these views of Williams may suggest, underlying his difference with the Puritans of Massachusetts Bay was a fundamental disagreement about how God works in human history. The providential view as set forth by Bradford led to a belief that God provides his people with blessings both spiritual and temporal. But Williams saw the Christian's lot as far different. This world is so set against God's ways that affliction is the usual fate. Williams protests that "fellowship with the Lord Jesus in his sufferings is sweeter than all the fellowship with sinners in all the profits, honors, and pleasures of this present world." He continues, "The portion of Christ's followers (like his own, and both like a woman in travail) [is] pain and sorrow, yea, poverty and persecution. . . ."[11]

Just as the individuals within the covenant of grace were considered the recipients of God's special care, the Puritans believed that God's providence guided a people who as a commonwealth were in covenant with him. Perry Miller pointed out the implications of this social covenant by comparing its fruits with those of the covenant of grace: "A group exists only in this world: it does not migrate *in toto* to heaven; both saints and sinners leave their earthly community behind, along with their clothes and property. Hence the relation of God to a community is not internal but external and 'foederall.' It has to do with conduct here and now, with visible success or tangible failure. Secondly, since a society cannot be rewarded in heaven for its obedience (whereas an individual may suffer torments here but receive endless compensation hereafter), and cannot be punished in hell (a reprobate may prosper all his life, but suffer throughout eternity), it must perforce contract with the Almighty for external ends. Its obedience, in short, means prosperity, its disobedience means war, epidemic, or ruin." This kind of thinking, that God would judge the commonwealth by its collective godliness or sinfulness, was in keeping with the notion that Massachusetts was a new Israel devoted to the observation of all of God's laws. In Massachusetts it was the magistrate's task to punish violations of the Ten Commandments, even the specifically religious first table, the first four commandments. As town and commonwealth records show, a great deal of time was taken up with dealing with the Sabbath-breakers and profane swearers. But Williams argued that these were none of the state's concern. To make such religious matters civil concerns would not make men in any meaningful way better; it would at best make them into hypocrites.[12]

History remembers the debate between Williams and John Cotton because of their disagreement on the question of religious toleration. In the debate Cotton argued that the officers of a Christian commonwealth should punish those who reject religious truth both because the state should protect the church from disturbance and because on fundamental points of doctrine and worship the Bible is so clear that truth is knowable. Thus once a person is shown the truth, he cannot claim the right to reject it for the sake of his conscience. On the contrary, to do so would be to sin against one's conscience. Williams was much more skeptical. He believed that persecution is likely to prevent men from embracing the truth:

howsoever they lay this down as an infallible conclusion that all heresy is against light of conscience, yet (to pass by the discussion of the nature of heresy, in which respect it may so be that even themselves may be found heretical, yea, and that in fundamentals) how do all idolaters, after light presented and exhortations powerfully pressed, either Turks or pagans, Jews or antichristians, strongly even to the death hold fast (or rather are held fast by) their delusions. Yea, God's people themselves, being deluded and captivated, are strongly confident even against some fundamentals, especially of worship, and yet not against the light but according to the light or eye of a deceived conscience.

The truth that was so strikingly clear, according to Cotton, even to the unregenerate, was for Williams hard for even God's saints to embrace.[13]

Probably the most appealing aspect of early New England Puritanism was its idealism and its innovativeness. Based on a profoundly felt need for the pure worship of God, this New England Puritanism led to the creation of a vigorous new state on the shores of a wilderness. The leaders of this state committed themselves, by covenant, to do God's will. But as Williams's critique of this experiment shows, there was another side to the colony. If it was based on innovative ideas, it was not consistent, not wholly idealistic. It had a conservative, compromising cast as well, or soon developed one.[14]

Roger Williams's controversy with Massachusetts points up some vital truths about Puritan orthodoxy. They may be summarized as follows:

1. God's fundamental truth is known; departures from it should be punished if instruction in truth is rejected. This conservative position Williams found narrowly and prematurely dogmatic, one

that makes oversimple the search for truth and can create only hypocrisy.

2. Massachusetts is a new Israel, where church and state live in harmonious obedience to God's laws. This position Williams found naive, insufficiently aware of the sinfulness of this world.

3. Massachusetts has created pure churches by limiting church membership to visible saints and permitting only them to receive the Lord's Supper. This semi-separatist position Williams found wrong because it prescribes still that saints and sinners shall worship together.

4. Massachusetts separated the functions of church and state, though both were conceived to have their authority from God and both sought to do God's will. Williams argued that the separation was insufficient because the state can have no concern with religious matters; Christianity is wholly concerned with the life of the spirit, with which the state has nothing to do.

5. Massachusetts Puritanism taught that since God's covenant with man is a continuing one, the covenant of grace established with Adam continues to the present day. This sense of continuity Williams considered confused since it failed to distinguish the Christian from the Jew or Old Testament worldliness from New Testament spirituality.

II   *Anne Hutchinson*

In the controversy with Williams, the standing order of Massachusetts was almost fully unified in opposition to one man, who remained something of an outsider. Winthrop, Cotton, the majority of the ministers, the General Court—all were opposed to Williams. When finally he left for Rhode Island, only a few followers went with him. A second body of dissenters, the Antinomians, was much larger, and the Antinomian Crisis had more powerful repercussions within the Puritan commonwealth because the controversy involved John Cotton himself, pitted against several of the leading ministers of the colony; it involved as well Sir Henry Vane, the youthful new governor, another minister, and many influential Bostonians.[15]

The controversy has not been well understood because its context is difficult to reconstruct. It is known that during the 1630s as large numbers of Englishmen migrated to New England, Puritan ministers were excited by the possibilities that lay before them. The dramatic migration was making possible the creation of what Winthrop called "a city on a hill," to which the world might look for a model of the kingdom of God on earth. History was entering a final phase when God's work of redemption was to be completed. In this context, a question that was inevitably asked was, What was Christ's kingdom on earth to be like? The answer, according to most of the Bay ministers, was that it would be a restoration of the paradise that Adam lost. What was the new man, the redeemed man, to be? The answer, according to most of the ministers, was that he was to be in the image of God: he was to be as Adam had been before the Fall. The restoration of individual fallen men that was to take place was much like the process that men could already experience, through the grace that brought regeneration.[16]

Thomas Shepard explained: "Those that are renewed to Adam's image in their measure have according to that measure power to act, or in those graces power to act, for he [Adam] had power so to do. Every creature in the world had a Law of Nature to carry them to their end, and so were carried to it. But Adam had a Law of Divinity whereby he . . . was enabled by God to carry himself to that image in part." Christ's grace permits man to be what Adam had been. "What hath the Lord done but opened the way to the tree of life and let you into Paradise again?" Shepard emphasized the point, clarified it, reinforced it: "The end of the minister is to bring us to the unity of faith in a perfect state" (Ephesians 4:13). He added, "Therefore faith shall not cease when ministers shall, and that perfect man shall come." Only this perfect man, this new Adam, is worthy of salvation, declared Shepard. "No man can stand before God but by perfect holiness, but by doing whatever the Law requires." Even in heaven, after Judgment Day, the saints will be as Adam was. He concluded, "Perfect subjection" to the Law "is the happiness of saints in Heaven."[17]

Opposed to this vision of the regenerate was the concept that John Cotton brought with him to America. (Considering the leading role that Cotton played in the early history of the commonwealth, it is surprising how often his opinion differed from those of his fellow ministers.) Cotton found "a broad difference between our sanctification and that of Adam's, in which he neither lived by faith nor put forth any act of an heart repenting and turning to the Lord." Cotton agreed that the converted were remade in the image of God, but not in the image of God as found in Adam but as found in Christ: "As our sanctification is the new man created in us after the image of God, so after the image of Christ especially. . . . .And our likeness to him in his death and resurrection consisteth in dying to sin and to this world and to ourselves, and in living unto Christ."[18]

Another difference between Cotton and the other ministers was their views on the question of preparation. Could fallen, sinful man do anything to seek his own salvation? Cotton's answer was a definite NO. The other ministers, notably Shepard and Bulkeley, preached that men can take certain steps to prepare themselves for salvation. Shepard warned his hearers: "Do not say, 'I am not able to come [to Christ] and therefore am not called.' No more are you able to attend the rules of the moral law. Yet you look upon them as appertaining to you, and because you cannot do them, you entreat the Lord to enable you, and so because you cannot come, you should look up to the Lord to draw you. And verily, many times the great reason why the Lord doth not draw you is because you do not deeply consider that he doth really and affectionately call you." Men may prepare for God's grace, Shepard argued, by many means, by prayer, penitence, contrition, humiliation.[19]

John Cotton was suspicious of such self-help doctrine. "Reserving due honor to such gracious and precious saints as may be otherwise minded," he politely noted, "I confess I do not discern that the Lord worketh and giveth any saving preparation till he give union with Christ, for if the Lord do any saving qualification before Christ, then the soul may be in the state of salvation before Christ, and that seemeth to be prejudicial unto the grace and truth of Jesus Christ." While other preachers offered the promises of the Bible as an inducement to faith, Cotton was strongly opposed to anything savoring of voluntarism: "Take heed you do not close with promises before you have Jesus Christ. Especially take heed you make not use of promises to a qualification to give you your part in Jesus Christ. . . . Do not turn them upside down beyond the scope and intendement of the covenant of grace. . . . Trust not unto every leaning of your souls upon conditional promises, for so you may build upon a covenant of works, and in the end you and your covenant will fail together."[20]

Although some ministers noted these differences in theology and preaching techniques, probably little would have come of them had it not been for Anne Hutchinson. In England Mrs. Hutchinson had lived not far from John Cotton's parish at Boston, Lincolnshire. She was a devout woman, particularly fond of hearing sermons. She found John Cotton to be a man who could meet her needs, and she became his devoted admirer. She supplemented the religious guidance that he provided with that of her brother-in-law, the Reverend John Wheelwright. But Wheelwright was silenced for nonconformity in 1632, and in 1633 Cotton left for America. A year later, guided by the spirit (she claimed), Anne Hutchinson followed him—with her husband and twelve children. In the new Boston she established herself as a competent nurse and midwife. Her religious interests led her to provide spiritual advice to the women she cared for. In time she drew a circle of women around her to hear her rehearse the sermons of her admired John Cotton, a circle that grew until it included both men and women, upwards of sixty in number. Cotton found the meetings valuable; he wrote later that "these private conferences did well to water the seed publicly sown."[21]

As her meetings or conferences grew, Mrs. Hutchinson widened her concern to include discussions of the teachings of other ministers. She emphasized the difference between Cotton's teaching and that of others, and she labelled "legalist" the preaching of ministers such as Shepard and Cotton's colleague at the Boston church, John Wilson. "Legalist" meant that they taught the importance of the Law, that one could prove he had been saved by his ability to lead a righteous life. For her, this was preaching a covenant of works, not grace. One of the appeals of Mrs. Hutchinson's teaching was that she offered a less rigidly moralistic kind of religion than that favored by most of the ministers as well as by the magistrates, whose position as guardians of public virtue was made easier by the teaching that godliness was accompanied by high moral standards. Those ministers whose doctrine she condemned soon heard of her meetings and her teachings, for she attracted church members from other towns than Boston. The ministers saw a possible connection between her teaching and that of her much admired John Cotton. What she was discussing interested nearly everybody, for stricter requirements for admission to church membership had recently been established, and there seems to have been a sudden cessation of the work of the Spirit, though conversions had until recently been very common. The result was a mood of religious anxiety.

Because of their concern, the ministers conferred in October 1636 with Cotton and John Wheelwright, who had recently arrived in Boston, and for a time it appeared that they were in sufficient agreement on doctrine to avoid controversy. But Cotton insisted that the person of the Holy Spirit dwelt within the regenerate; he rejected the more extreme form of the same doctrine, that the regenerate have actual union with the Holy Spirit. At the same time that the ministers were attempting to create harmony, Mrs. Hutchinson's followers were attempting to gain power. Being very doubtful of the orthodoxy of John Wilson, they promoted the candidacy of John Wheelwright as an additional minister for the Boston church. Their efforts failed, partly because Winthrop strenuously objected, partly because it was difficult to justify having three ministers. The disputes continued, however, with Sir Henry Vane (elected governor in 1636) advocating Mrs. Hutchinson's position. Cotton and Wilson came into sharp dispute, and some of the Bostonians attempted an official condemnation by the church of Wilson's doctrine. It was not until John Wheelwright advocated in a sermon a battle "against the enemies of the Lord" who advocated a covenant of works that the question was fully joined. Wheelwright was cited by the General Court for sedition, he being more vulnerable than Cotton. The Bostonian followers of Mrs. Hutchinson now told the Court that religious opinions were none of the Court's business. So a synod of ministers was called, and a survey of questionable doctrines in circulation was collected. Among the more than eighty that were identified were some far more radical than anything that Cotton had taught, though his doctrines may well have been their inspiration. For example, Winthrop lists these: "Sin in a child of God must never trouble him." "No Christian must be pressed to duties of holiness." "An hypocrite may have Adam's graces that he had in innocency." In teachings as extreme as these the Hutchinsonians were indeed Antinomians who held that the moral law does not apply to Christians. The synod condemned all of the doctrines collected.[22]

Mrs. Hutchinson's doctrines followed from John Cotton's teaching on the nature of regeneration. Like him, she emphasized that it was through faith that one knew he was saved. This doctrine was consistent with Calvinism and the logic of Reformed orthodoxy. Cotton explained how "the Spirit of God taking possession in our hearts and working . . . faith in us, thereby we submit unto the Lord, and this is faith in Jesus Christ, that maketh us one with Christ, for our effectual calling bringeth us to be with him." This divine indwelling, Cotton insisted, was the essence of conversion. Mrs. Hutchinson emphasized religious experience, and ultimately she declared she had the benefit of private revelation. Winthrop's report on the episode notes that Mrs. Hutchinson "walked by such a rule as cannot stand with the peace of any state." If guidance by private revelation were permitted "in one thing," he wrote, it "must be admitted a rule in all things." In a commonwealth that believed that the Word of God was the absolute authority, Mrs. Hutchinson's way was profoundly threatening.[23]

Mrs. Hutchinson's cultivation of private revelations was a natural outgrowth of Puritanism. Historically Puritans had been those who rejected the formal, external worship of the Church of England in favor of an experiential knowledge of God. This semimystical side of Puritanism is suggested by the titles of Hooker's works *The Soules Ingrafting into Christ* (1637) and *The Soules Possession of Christ* (1638). It was particularly identified with the Puritan preaching of Richard Sibbes, who had converted John Cotton; Sibbes was in fact Cotton's model. Those who yearned for religious experience were attracted to New England. Roger Clapp, a Dorchester layman, recalled in his last years the atmosphere of early Massachusetts:

Oh how did men and women, young and old, pray for grace, beg for Christ in those days. And it was not in vain. Many were converted, and others established in believing. Many joined unto the several churches where they lived, confessing their faith publicly, and showing before all the assembly their experiences of the workings of God's spirit in their hearts to bring them to Christ, which many hearers found very much good by, to help them to try their own hearts, and to consider how it was with them, whether any work of God's spirit were wrought in their hearts or no. Oh the many tears that have been shed in Dorchester meeting house at such times, both by those that have declared God's work on their souls, and also by those that heard them. In those days God, even our own God, did bless New England.

Such religious enthusiasm was regarded with suspicion by those in power because in a new commonwealth, without strong traditions, whatever might create instability was dangerous. That there was reason to be wary is suggested by a comment of one of the Hutchinsonians, as recorded by Edward Johnson: " 'Come along with me,' says one of them, 'I'll bring you to a woman that preaches better gospel than any of your blackcoats that have been at the Ninneversity, a woman of another kind of spirit, who hath had many revelations of things to come, and for my part,' saith he, 'I had rather hear such a one that speaks from the mere motion of the Spirit, without any study at all, than any of your learned scholars, although they may be fuller of Scripture.' " This kind of anti-establishment, anti-intellectual attitude eventually flourished into the Inner Light doctrine of the Quakers.[24]

In May 1637 John Winthrop was once again elected governor, succeeding Sir Henry Vane. Winthrop was a vigorous opponent of the Hutchinsonians, although they were members of his own church. Though now condemned by the synod, Antinomian doctrines continued to be aired at the Boston church until the General Court banished the leaders of the Hutchinsonians. The climax of the whole affair was the banishment and excommunication of Mrs. Hutchinson. John Cotton himself agreed to tone down those aspects of his teaching that differed from that of the other ministers, but he never admitted to being less than orthodox.

The effects of the Antinomian controversy on American Puritanism were manifold. First, the dispute disrupted for a time the harmony that the colony was cultivating. Deputy-Governor Thomas Dudley explained that "About three years ago we were all in peace. Mrs. Hutchinson from that time she hath made a disturbance, and some that came over with her in the ship did inform me what she was as soon as she was landed. . . . Now it appears by this woman's meetings that Mrs. Hutchinson hath so forestalled the minds of many by their resort to her meeting that now she hath a potent party in the country." Cotton himself was regarded with great suspicion, and he and "many other sincerely godly brethren" of his church in Boston planned to move to New Haven, or so Cotton himself reported. (New Haven, a strictly orthodox colony, had just been established.) Some forty Boston families, including influential ones, did leave the colony, many going to tolerant Rhode Island. A contemporary, who blamed Sir Henry Vane for much of the trouble, wrote of the sparks kindled among the colonists "which many ages will not be able to extinguish."[25]

Second, the controversy helped create in Massachusetts a more authoritarian atmosphere. Winthrop tells of preachers being attacked in public by the Hutchinsonians for the sermons they preached, a practice that the newly developed Congregationalism did something to encourage. Now eager to prevent any future uprising among the laity, the ministers limited the democratic tendency within Congregationalism. Orthodoxy was more precisely defined, and aberrations were regarded with suspicion. The synod officially warned against the questioning of ministers by the laity and the holding of private meetings. The very fact that the extremist

Hutchinsonians and Roger Williams were exiled made dissent much less attractive.[26]

Third, the religious spirit of Massachusetts was profoundly changed. Religious enthusiasm was now seen to be potentially disruptive. The doctrines preached by Thomas Shepard became dominant: in place of a warm pietism, preachers increasingly emphasized rigid morality, and they made more of man's moral capacities. While they did not deny God's sovereignty or the irresistibleness of His grace, they emphasized that the conversion process required action from man. Conversions became rarer, and many ministers began to blame the unconverted. This new attitude can be seen, for example, in a work by the man who was to succeed John Cotton in Boston: John Norton (1606 - 1663). In *The Orthodox Evangelist* (London, 1654), Norton argued that men are not totally corrupt, unable to act. They are reasonable, and "The rule of the reasonable creature is the moral law. In the government of the reasonable creature (one must observe) an obediential power, that is, a capacity of the creature to become subject unto the will of the creator. . . . God prescribes unto the reasonable creature a rule" (pp. 103 - 104). A believing Christian is in Norton's words "not only a subject but also an efficient co-working cause" of his "own salvation" (p. 260). In this quasi-Arminian scheme, God does "not work savingly upon us as upon stocks or senseless creatures"; rather he recognizes distinctively human capacities. "Man is a reasonable creature," and in dealing with him "God proceedeth by way of arguments . . ." (pp. 212 - 213). If conversion preaching was frequently unsuccessful, the blame could be laid on the unchurched.[27]

III   *The Cambridge Platform*

The ecclesiastical polity of Massachusetts Bay Puritanism crystallized as a result of the controversies that threatened to destroy the commonwealth; this polity is described in many writings—by Cotton, Hooker, Richard Mather, John Davenport. None of these writings, however, had official status, though Hooker's *Survey of the Summe of Church Discipline* (1648) had been approved by a group of New England ministers. Nevertheless, there was generally uniformity in the government of Massachusetts and Connecticut churches, though a few churches followed presbyterian practice insofar as they did not limit membership strictly and did not give power to the membership. There was, clearly, a congregational system in operation, and it was not uniformly popular. In the year 1646, with Presbyterians in power in England, a group of solid citizens under the leadership of Dr. Robert Child, a physician, protested to the General Court of Massachusetts Bay that the New England Way violated their rights as Englishmen and gave formal notice that unless they were given satisfaction, they would protest to Parliament.[28]

Specifically, the protesters took up three grievances:

1. That the government of Massachusetts Bay was not according to the laws of England;

2. That civil liberty, freemanship, and office-holding was denied many able people;

3. That church membership was restricted to those who would accept church covenants, which they judged to lack Biblical authority, and that nevertheless they were required to attend sermons, even to witness baptism being administered to other men's children though denied to their own.[29]

The protesters were chiefly Boston merchants, attracted to New England because of its potential for commercial and industrial development. But their dissatisfactions with the Puritan limitations placed on the franchise were shared by members of the younger generation, and they addressed their appeal to the deputies in the General Court, many of whom felt that the magistrates had too much power. But few in Massachusetts wanted Parliament to intervene in the colony's internal affairs, and the magistrates were able to rally opposition to the protesting petitioners by citing the danger of loss of Massachusetts sovereignty.[30]

Even before the protest was received, Massachusetts secular and spiritual leaders judged that there was need for a uniform, obligatory policy on church government, especially since Congregationalism enjoyed support from the most powerful political leaders. Therefore a synod was called to make a definitive statement that the General Court could approve. The Court's call recognized that England was in turmoil and suggested that the peace currently being experienced in New England might not long continue. The particular concern was expected to be baptism: Who was entitled to it? This question was not, however, squarely faced, because there was no general agreement about it. Not until the 1660s was the vexed question of baptism fully explored.[31]

The synod met in 1646 and again in 1647. Before it finished its deliberations, the court added to its responsibilities another: to prepare a statement "touching the doctrinal points of religion." Since no significant doctrinal differences existed between the New England Puritans and the Old England Presbyterians who had prepared through their instrument the Westminster Assembly a Confession of Faith, the New Englanders accepted it. The *Platform of Church Discipline*, better known as the Cambridge Platform, was the chief fruit of the synod's deliberations. It was widely but not uniformly accepted, and the General Court did not make it mandatory. The reasons for this cooling off of ardor for uniformity seem to be two. First, there was some opposition, especially in Boston, to the concept of a synod. Second, and much more important, the Presbyterians in England had lost power to the Army, in which Independents (the Congregationalists of England) were in control. Now Parliament's instrument, the Commissioners for Plantations, reported that they did not intend "to encourage any appeals from Massachusetts Bay" but to recognize the rights of jurisdiction of the Puritan commonwealth in the New World.[32]

The Platform's codification is best seen as the consensus that had been evolved by the Puritans. In eighteen years Congregationalism had been solidly established. Here was the rationale. While acceptance of every article was not required, the document nevertheless suggests what the Puritans generally believed to be the norm that was now established. The Platform's seventeen chapters are full of precise definitions. They establish that churches are created by visible covenants. They describe church government and the election of officers, their ordination and maintenance, admission of members to church discipline; they explain how synods may be called to determine controversies. Chapter XVII explains what power the civil magistrate is given in ecclesiastical matters. The civil government and the church are described as coordinate, "the one being helpful unto the other in their distinct and due administrations." The magistrate's aim is not merely to establish justice and peace but to create goodness. Specifically, the civil authority is to restrain and punish "idolatry, blasphemy, heresy, venting corrupt and pernicious opinions that destroy the foundation, open contempt of the word preached, profanation of the Lord's Day, disturbing the peaceable administration and exercise of the worship and holy things of God and the like."[33]

The synod's definition of Congregationalism was carefully drawn and represented, probably, a genuine consensus of Massachusetts ministers and church members. But the creation of these formulations, with their rigid conception of orthodoxy, made it difficult for Puritans to react effectively to new situations. The churches eventually failed to meet the challenges presented by changing conditions.[34]

In its first two decades Puritanism in New England was shaped by the ideals of the founders—but also by circumstance, by the need to maintain itself in the face of opposition and by the necessity to compromise. To maintain some semblance of a unified community, and something of the Puritan principle of pure and covenanted churches, Puritan leaders made their commonwealth more rigid and intolerant. They had created a new society that in many ways was attractive, certainly innovative. They were much less successful at preserving and maintaining what they had created.

CHAPTER 4

The Sons of the Founders

" " G OD sifted a whole nation that he might send choice grain over into this wilderness." So wrote William Stoughton in 1670. The self-selected founders of New England were bold, energetic folk, confident and open to new ideas. Such qualities, always rare, are remarkable when one realizes that many of the leaders were middle-aged when they crossed to the New World: Winthrop was forty-two, Hooker forty-seven, Cotton forty-nine, and Bulkeley fifty-two. Congregationalism and representative government were established in New England early because talented, able, and forceful people demanded a role in government, in both church and state.[1]

I *Stress between Generations*

The innovative founders of New England soon created a stable society, one that not merely survived: New England flourished. By the end of the first decade, eighteen towns were settled in Massachusetts Bay, with additional towns in Connecticut. (Roger Williams and his followers were well established in Rhode Island, but the Massachusetts Bay colonists could claim no credit for their successes.) The threats that the colonists had met, especially that of the Hutchinsonians, had caused a conservative reaction, and the Commonwealth of Massachusetts Bay became rigid, exclusive, intolerant, and isolationist. New traditions are more likely to meet opposition than old, and the men of the second generation inevitably found their once innovative but now arch-conservative fathers very demanding. Since the fathers were unusually long-lived, the repression of the young was continued for a long time, with results that are predictable.

The first generation considered the younger—simply because it was younger—as threatening the ideals to which they had become devoted. The children could not be expected to believe that the institutions and the mores that the fathers had created in the wilderness were now permanently fixed, or at least the fathers seem to have feared that they would permit change and, specifically, backsliding. S. E. Morison characterized the gap between the generations by describing the two John Winthrops: "John Winthrop the elder is severe, dignified, introspective, medieval; John Winthrop the younger is eager, outgoing, genial, responsive, modern. The younger man was broad-minded, but never sounded the depth of religious experience as his father had done; the elder had seen much of life, but only from the angle of a Puritan magistrate." The son of the founder of Springfield, Massachusetts, was also very different from his father. The younger, John Pynchon, according to Morison, "was zealous in upholding the religion of his time, but he does not appear to have had any of the polemic and controversial spirit of his father. He was too eminently practical to enter into the discussion of the different points of theology" as his father had done. John was a businessman. In general the second generation seemed to the first to be frivolous. The General Court of Massachusetts Bay noted the growth of "sensuality" and referred to "the sad face on the rising generation." To preserve what they had created, the fathers kept their children from power as long as possible. A chief instrument that they used was the land, most of which they controlled. Sons had to wait long for their inheritance and independence. Average marriage ages were high, twenty-seven for men and twenty-five for women during the second half of the seventeenth century.[2]

Another limiting factor was church admission policy. Under John Cotton's leadership, as we have seen, the first generation established high admission standards for membership: only those who could provide substantial evidence that they had been converted could be admitted. Sons had to pass tests not yet invented when their fathers had joined the church. One historian has suggested that most men of the second generation "could not experience a psychologically convincing conversion so long as their fathers were still alive to provide thunderous comparisons from the 1630s." Another historian, Edmund S. Morgan, noted, "The Puritans had in fact moved the church so far from the world that it would no longer fit the biological facts of life. Had they been willing to move it a little farther still, by forming monasteries instead of churches, they might have concentrated on their own purity and left to others the task of supplying the church with new members."[3]

Church membership meant more than enjoying a certain religious status. By means of a series of political decisions, church members enjoyed political privileges not available to nonmembers. Under John Winthrop's leadership, the General Court of Massachusetts Bay had limited the franchise to church members, and later the Court ruled that no church could be organized without the permission of the majority of the existing churches and the approval of the civil magistrates. By the end of the 1630s, great importance had been given to church membership, with no dissident competing churches permitted to disrupt the status quo. Church membership was necessary for first-class political citizenship, and fewer and fewer people were qualifying for membership.[4]

In the 1640s English Puritans frequently attacked the policy of restricting membership. John Cotton, as spokesman for the system, was called to answer the charge that the New England churches excluded "many thousand Christians, whom they dare not deny to be truly religious, of all the privileges of the church." Cotton could only reply that everyone was allowed to attend all services and that only the Lord's Supper was limited to church members. He chose not to refer to the implications of church membership in the body politic: the creation of a large number of second-class citizens.[5]

II *The Half-Way Covenant*

Time and change led to theological and ecclesiastical adjustments. While Puritanism may appear to have been an extreme form of religious thought, it was in fact a compromise that was always in danger of falling apart. Nothing in the history of New England Puritanism demonstrates its paradoxical nature better than the situation that led to the "half-way" covenant, a compromise made necessary by earlier compromises and by the strict standards of admission to church membership. The principles adopted by the synod of 1662 are an important modification of the principles of the founders.

According to covenant theology, the covenant "which God hath made with his faithful people to be a God unto them and to their seed" is sealed by baptism. That sacrament was available only to those who believed that God had called them and to the seed of such believers. In baptism parents "give up . . . their seed to the Lord" and agree to train up "their children in the ways of his covenant." As a seal, baptism simply confirmed "something that was before," something there by virtue of church membership of the parents. That "something" was ill defined. According to the Cambridge Platform of 1648, baptized children were "in a more hopeful way of attaining regenerating grace" than others because "they are in covenant with God." On the other hand, no orthodox Puritan believed that baptism was necessary for salvation. It was chiefly a means by which the minister, in exchange for administering an important Christian ritual, could encourage both parents and children to accept religious obligations.[6]

Baptism did not provide salvation; it *probably*, very *likely* indicated that God's saving grace would come in due time. Baptism was taken seriously because it was Biblical, because it was traditional, because it had a place in covenantal thought, and because the Antinomians, the Hutchinsonians, had scoffed at it, finding it insignificant compared with the immediate experience of the spirit. The early New England Puritans assumed that most baptized children would grow up to experience conversion and would thereby be eligible for church membership. Here is how John Cotton had put it: ". . . the children of believers do come on themselves to believe by reason of the covenant of grace which God hath made with believers and their seed, for by that covenant he hath promised to write the law of faith (as of all other saving graces) in their hearts, that they also may come in God's time and way to enjoy all the other saving privileges of the covenant, as did their fathers before them."[7]

As already noted, the founders of New England saw to their enormous disappointment that relatively few of their children became church members. Grace was supposed to descend by means of the covenant to descendants of visible saints. It did not. In the 1660s the minister Jonathan Mitchell complained that "the Lord hath not set up churches only that a few old Christians may keep one another warm while they live, and then carry away the church into the cold grave when they die." But, as Robert Pope has written, "The new test put beyond the grasp of many what had been within the reach of most men of good will." Something had gone wrong, perhaps because of the effort to keep the churches as pure as possible. Were the churches to die? What was the status of those adults who were not church members though they had been baptized as children? And were the children of these adults entitled to baptism? In 1662 the Massachusetts General Court called a synod to look into the matter.[8]

The synod focused its discussion on baptism, but the underlying question was the role of the churches. Baptism was conceived as the instrument by which the power of the churches could be extended, for it gave the church disciplinary rights over those in covenant. The key proposition adopted by the synod put it this way: "Church members who were admitted in minority, understanding the doctrine of faith and publicly professing their assent thereto, not scandalous in life, and *solemnly owning the covenant before the church*, wherein they give up themselves and their children to the Lord, and subject themselves to the government of Christ in the church, their children are to be baptized." In exchange for a kind of membership for their children through baptism, the parents committed themselves to the discipline of the church. The parents "are personally under discipline and are liable to church censures in their own person." Thus what has been conceived of as a liberalizing of the rules was in fact a way of extending the jurisdiction of the church.[9]

Opponents of the new doctrine argued that it polluted and profaned the churches, that the leaders of the synod had committed apostasy. In fact, the half-way covenant gave new meaning to the church covenant and eroded the old Calvinist doctrine of total depravity. It gave adults and children "half-way" membership in the church in exchange for their best efforts to lead Christian lives, even though they presumably lacked the saving grace that was a requirement for full membership and admission to the Lord's Supper. The ideals of the synod were slowly adopted everywhere. In time, many ministers felt justified in teaching that "owning the covenant" was a religious duty that could be demanded of everyone, even though they could not meet the requirements of full membership.[10]

Baptism and owning the covenant became means by which the churches attempted to remain vital. Preachers made much of the obligations of those who had been baptized. They called upon their whole congregation to reform, for, as the 1679 "reforming synod" declared, "Solemn and explicit renewal of the covenant is a scripture expedient for reformation." The churches of the last third of the century were not the voluntary communities of those who believed that they had been called to sainthood; they were churches of birthright members who were made to feel a sense of obligation. In some towns only a handful of people attended the Lord's Supper, until the grandchildren of the founders, men like Cotton Mather, felt obliged to tell the baptized that they were sinners if they *failed* to receive the Lord's Supper. Mather pleaded with his congregation, "There is no escaping or avoiding of great sin without coming to the table of the Lord." The attempt to institutionalize the vision of the pure church of visible saints had failed. Instead, the churches of New England Puritanism now sought to maintain some kind of control over the community, over the indifferent and over the pious, who might demand so much of themselves that they would not dare to apply for church membership.[11]

III   *The New Jerusalem and the Jeremiad*

Other difficulties plagued the second generation. Calamities, natural and otherwise, filled the already anxious heirs with self-doubt. The Indian Wars, especially King Philip's War of the 1670s, the revocation of the colony's charter, and eventually the witchcraft outbreak caused New Englanders to question themselves. Had they done wrong that God's wrath was being so poured out on them? The sovereign God who controlled the universe must be punishing his people. It must be that they were inadequate sons. Eleazar Mather, son of the founder Richard, well described how the second generation looked upon themselves when he wrote in 1671 that his generation was "like a company of children that is driven out to sea, may be it may come to shore, but in greater danger to sink or drown than otherwise." To stir up this generation, preachers catalogued the sins of omission and commission that they found to characterize the times, then threatened providential judgment unless reformation ensued. Pulpit denunciations came to characterize an entire era.[12]

Principal among the charges against the second generation, inevitably, was that they had abandoned the founders' design. Finding in retrospect that New England's creation had been part of God's plan, that its role in human history was intended to be climactic, the preacher envisioned the founders' task to have been the creation of a New Jerusalem. This idea had been frequently expressed, chiefly as a pious hope, by such leaders as John Cotton. The founders meant that they had the opportunity to create a pure society. Increase Mather could declare in 1679, "Where was there ever a place so like unto new Jerusalem as New England hath been?" New England's early years became in retrospect a golden age. Mather described New England as "a type and emblem of the new-Jerusalem" that was to flourish in the millenium, when Christ would reign on earth for a thousand years. Urian Oakes, son of a founder, saw Massachusetts as "a little model of the Kingdom of Christ upon earth."[13]

The great exemplar for the second and third generation preachers was the Old Testament prophet Jeremiah; their sermons were "jeremiads." In his memorable essay, "Declension in a Bible Commonwealth," Perry Miller described how

on the great occasions of communal life, when the body politic met in solemn conclave to consider the state of society, the one kind of sermon it attended was not an exposition of doctrine, not a description of holiness or of grace, not a discourse on what had once been the preoccupation of New England, the reformation of polity, but instead was a jeremiad in which the sins of New England were tabulated over and over again, wherein the outward judgments which God had already ifflicted were held to presage what he would increase in violence unless New England hastened to restore the model of holiness. . . . Fifty years after the Great Migration, the literary form in which the New England mind found its most appropriate expression was the jeremiad.[14]

As Miller suggests, the jeremiads are remarkably similar in both form and content. A good sample is one of the most famous, the 1670 election sermon preached by Samuel Danforth entitled *A Brief Recognition of New Englands Errand into the Wilderness*. Minister at Roxbury since 1650, a graduate of Harvard, Danforth had come to America in 1634 at the age of eight. He looked back at the early days of the Puritan commonwealth with complete admiration; in comparison with it he judged his own generation to be corrupt and degenerate. As a text, Danforth chose Matthew 11: 7-9, which begins, "What went ye forth to see?" After an exploration of the situation treated by the text, which describes John the Baptist, the austere prophet of true religion who had gone to live in the wilderness, and his followers, Danforth sets forth his doctrine: "Such as have sometime left their pleasant cities and habitations to enjoy the pure worship of God in a wilderness are apt to abate and cool in their affection thereunto; but then the Lord calls upon them seriously and thoroughly to examine themselves, what it was that drew them into the wilderness, and to consider that it was not the expectation of ludicrous levity nor of courtly pomp and delicacy, but of the free and clear dispensation of the Gospel and kingdom of God."[15]

After citing Biblical examples to demonstrate the doctrine and the traditional "reasons for the doctrine," the preacher arrives at

the heart of his message, the "uses." He finds that the people of
New England have forgotten what their errand was, and he reminds
them: "You have solemnly professed before God, angels, and men
that the cause of your leaving your country, kindred, and fathers'
houses and transporting yourselves with your wives, little ones, and
substance into this waste and howling wilderness, was your liberty
to walk in the faith of the Gospel with all good conscience according to the order of the Gospel, and your enjoyment of the pure
worship of God according to his institution without human mixtures
and impositions" (p. 65). He then draws a picture of the early days
of Massachusetts Bay, when religious zeal and moral purity were
everywhere to be found, when all considered themselves "blessed in
the enjoyment of a pious, learned, and orthodox ministry" (p. 66),
when heresies and new "revelations" were vigorously rejected.

Now instead of religious fervor, Danforth finds around him immorality and religious indifference, the causes of which he identifies
as unbelief and worldliness, despite the fact that New Englanders
had come "into these wild woods and deserts" for the sole purpose
of pure worship of God. Because New England has so neglected its
purpose, the God with whom New England has covenanted has
visited on the delinquents mildew, drought, storms, floods, earth-
quakes, and blazing stars. (All these New England had indeed experienced.) Moreover, God had removed, as punishment, many
valuable ministers from their work. To prevent further disasters and
calamities, Danforth asks in closing for "diligent attention to the
ministry of the Gospel" (p. 77). His final words are reassuring: New
Englanders know that if they devote themselves to God, they will
enjoy God's "promise of divine protection and preservation" (p.
77).

The idea that New England was in some way analogous to
Biblical Israel, that it was a New Israel, had several sources. First,
the Puritans could see that the founders, chosen people because
elected by God to salvation, had made an exodus to the wilderness
to establish by covenant a new society in which, as in ancient Israel,
leaders of both church and state sought to fulfill God's commands
cooperatively. Second, the younger generation, those whose lives
through early adulthood had been dominated by the heavy hands of
the founders, tended to be hero-worshippers. These men of the
1660s and 1670s believed that there were giants in the earth in those
earlier years. Joshua Scottow described the founders as "men of
God" who were "made partakers of the divine nature; Christ was

formed and visibly legible in them; they served God in houses of the first edition, without large chambers, or windows, ceiled with cedar, or painted with vermillion; a company of plain, pious, humble, and open-hearted Christians, called Puritans." Third, and perhaps most important, the Puritans came to see the founders' efforts in the context of providential history.[16]

The sophisticated approach to history of the second and third generations was based on typology, a way of reading both history and the Bible. Samuel Mather, son of a founder, defined what is meant by a type: "A type is some outward or sensible thing ordained of God under the Old Testament to represent and hold forth something of Christ in the New." (Mather devoted an entire book to the subject, *The Figures or Types of the Old Testament, by which Christ and Heavenly Things of the Gospel were Preached or Shadowed to the People of God of Old.*) The typologists based their exegetical theory on certain Biblical passages that emphasized parallels. Christ himself referred to Jonah's three days and nights in the whale as analogous to his three days and nights in the grave (Matthew 12:40). John made a parallel between Moses's serpent and Christ: "And as Moses lifted up the serpent in the wilderness, even so must the Son of man be lifted up" (John 3:14). The entire Epistle to the Hebrews is based on typology. It refers to "the law having a shadow of good things to come and not the very image of the things" (10:1). There the new covenant is described as analogous to the old; Christ is analogous to a high priest; the sacrifice of Christ replaces the burnt offerings of the past. This method of Biblical analyses led typologists to read the movement of history as being from adumbration and anticipation to reality, from the physical type to the spiritual antitype. Most Old Testament types were fulfilled, according to typologists, with the coming of Christ and his crucifixion, but some events, such as Moses's leading his people out of Egypt and into the Promised Land, had not had their complete fulfillment in Biblical history.[17]

Since all history was for the Puritans shaped by God's hand, all of history could be read typologically, as anticipation and fulfillment, and all of history was inevitably moving towards the complete fulfillment of God's will in the millennium prophesied in Chapter 20 of Revelation. But history could be read backward as well as forward; an event might be both the fulfillment of a prophecy and the prefiguration of a later, spiritual event. In this mode of thinking Israel was a type of New England and Israel's history anticipated

New England's. Israel was the precedent to which the Puritans looked; like Israel, New England was a covenanted community dedicated to God's purposes. These parallels were constantly set before the Puritans by the preaching sons of the founders.[18]

Increase Mather, the central figure of his age, son of a founder and a religious, political, and educational leader, was dominated by typological thought. As he examined Biblical history to understand the current events of his day, he saw that after the great leaders of Israel had led the Lord's people from the tyranny of Egypt into the wilderness, their successors had to contend with a backsliding, degenerating people whose corruptions caused God to punish them. Making the obvious application, Mather preached in a fast-day sermon, *The Day of Trouble is Near* (1671), that God "doth sometimes bring times of great trouble upon his own people." He saw his generation deeply divided, with disobedience rampant in families, in churches, and in the commonwealth. To avoid the coming awful judgment of God, he demanded repentance and reformation. When shortly afterwards, in the fall of 1675, King Philip's War broke out, the Massachusetts General Court saw the connection Mather had been making. They voted a series of laws intended to create the needed reforms.[19]

Another second-generation Puritan leader, son of the founder Israel Stoughton, was William Stoughton, who moved from preaching to politics and became governor in the late 1690s. In a 1668 election sermon he emphasized the covenant with God that bound the Puritans together: "Hath not the eye of the Lord beheld us laying *covenant-engagements* upon our selves?" He reminds his hearers of "our explicit ownings of, and covenantings with the Lord our God, laying this as a foundation stone in our building. . . ." Stoughton questions, "Whom hath the Lord more signally exalted than his people in this wilderness?" New England's history in the second half of the century could be read as a series of calamities, and, as Perry Miller has noted, "the jeremiad could make sense out of existence only as long as adversity was to be overcome."[20]

The preachers of the jeremiad thus created a myth of a golden age, from which the sons had dangerously departed. Earlier, at the end of the first decade, John Cotton had addressed to his congregation this resolve: "And therefore it is for us to do all the good we can, and to leave nothing to those that shall come after us, but to walk in the righteous steps of their forefathers. And therefore let us not leave, or give rest to our eyes, until as a family, church and commonwealth we have set a pattern of holiness to those that shall succeed us." John Oxenbridge warned, in 1673, "The first worthy planters they professed to erect and administer according to God. . . . But the bastard son will needs break to the ruin of himself and his partakers . . . ." He contrasted the present "degenerate and spurious generation" with "their faithful ancestors."[21]

The founders had indeed achieved much. But their children had far fewer creative opportunities, especially since nearly every Massachusetts Bay institution was considered to be fixed in its proper pattern. The feelings of inadequacy that the second generation suffered were intensified by significant changes in the context of the Puritan enterprise in New England. Back in England in 1643 the Long Parliament had convened the Westminster Assembly to determine what shape the reformed Church of England was to take as the Puritans moved into power, and Thomas Hooker, John Cotton, and John Davenport were all invited to attend. None went, but Cotton wrote *The Keyes of the Kingdom of Heaven* (1644), and Davenport, Hooker, Richard Mather, and John Norton all undertook written explanations of the New England Way to persuade the Assembly to adopt its example. Some Englishmen who had experienced the congregationalism created in the New World were available to the small group of English Congregationalists who attended the Assembly: former Governor Sir Henry Vane, Hugh Peter, and Thomas Welde, the latter two having been ordained in New England. But because the leaders of English Congregationalism were advocating religious tolerance, the example of New England was potentially embarrassing and better forgotten. The American experience went for naught in the important developments of the 1640s and 1650s in England, and afterwards Puritanism gave way as episcopacy and the Book of Common Prayer were reestablished in the Church of England. Henceforth, English Puritans were the dissenters: opportunities for power and influence were small.[22]

As a consequence the New Englanders had, in David Minter's phrase, "to reshape their heritage and redefine what they were about." The Puritans who had come to America had gone out on a limb, and now the limb had been sawed off. Like it or not, they were Americans. The jeremiad, the instrument by which the sons admitted their inadequacy, served as a means of role redefinition. Preached on public occasions such as election days and days set

aside by civil authorities for fasting and repentance or for thanksgiving, the jeremiad became the means by which the Puritans defined
themselves as still a dedicated people. Accepting the severe
judgments that the ministers dispensed became a way of accepting
the obligations that they felt they owed to the founders. They
acknowledged their failure to honor the founders' design—a design
doubtless much clearer in retrospect to the sons than it had ever
been to the fathers. By paying their respects to their fathers' mission, the second generation had some sense of having fulfilled their
obligations. In Minter's words, "they substituted the dedicated action of telling and retelling their inherited story for the dedicated
action of pursuing their inherited task." The retelling did not cease,
however, with the second generation. Given new force and clarity
by Cotton Mather and Jonathan Edwards, the myth of the golden
age, the legend of the founders' mission, contributed to the idea of
America's millennial role. The title of Samuel Baldwin's 1854
prophecy suggests how lasting was the influence of the jeremiad:
*Armageddon: Or, The Existence of the United States Foretold in
The Bible, Its . . . Expansion into the Millennial Republic, and Its
Dominion Over the Whole World.*[23]

Puritan leaders of the late seventeenth century did what they could
to retain power. The instruments used for control included the
jeremiad, invoking the covenant and baptismal vows, and recalling
the fathers' great achievements. All means, however, failed. The
churches of the Puritans were rapidly losing their influence. The excited piety of the 1630s was gone. The communion of the saints was
an outmoded ideal.

CHAPTER 5

Some Puritan Achievements

T HE creation of New England was doubtless the Puritans'
greatest achievement. The rapid growth of Puritan New
England was phenomenal. In 1643 "the United Colonies of New
England" (Massachusetts Bay, Plymouth, Connecticut, and New
Haven) was formed because "we are further dispersed upon the
seacoasts and rivers than was at first intended." In the same year,
New Englanders issued a progress report, *New Englands First
Fruits*. They could boast of having brought civilization into the
wilderness, a remarkable "maturity in a short time,"

having planted fifty towns and villages, built thirty or forty churches, and
more ministers' houses, a castle, a college, prisons, forts, cartways, causeys
many, and all these upon our own charge, no public hand reaching out any
help; having comfortable houses, gardens, orchards, grounds fenced, corn
fields, etc., and such a form and face of a commonwealth appearing in all
the plantation that strangers from other parts, seeing how much is done in
so few years, have wondered at God's blessing on our endeavors.

New England Puritanism produced not only New England; it had
significant intellectual and literary accomplishments of which it
could boast, and these accomplishments reveal much about
Puritanism.[1]

I *The Eloquence of Thomas Hooker*

New England might well never have come into existence had it
not been for the powerful preaching of its leading ministers, who attracted to the New World men and women hungry for the spiritual
food that sermons provided. It was John Cotton's preaching that attracted Anne Hutchinson to America, and a group who identified
themselves as "Mr. Hooker's Company" migrated to America in
1632 with the understanding that Thomas Hooker would join them,

as he did the following year. The preachers who came to New England were among England's best, at a time when preaching had reached a very high level of excellence. Of the many notable preachers of the early years of New England whose sermons have survived, those of Thomas Hooker are regarded as having particular literary value. They live for the modern reader, who can find much to appreciate and even admire in the best of them. Hooker was probably the greatest preacher of American Puritanism.[2]

Many of the sermons that Hooker preached, in England and America, were later published. Twenty-seven volumes, some consisting of single sermons, some of a series, were published in the seventeenth century. Of these a goodly number deal with Hooker's specialty, the morphology of religious conversion. In these sermons Hooker provides a discussion of how the process takes place, what its steps consist of, how God manipulates those He would call to sainthood without raping their wills. The sermons that describe the process are themselves intended to be the means by which God calls those to whom Hooker is preaching. They are diagnostic and potentially curative. Much of Hooker's skill as a preacher stems from his understanding of human behavior. While he was exceptionally tough-minded and saw conversion, true conversion, as the result of a long and often painful process, he convinces the reader that he knows what he is discussing, that the mental processes are familiar territory to him. He was persuasive because he spoke in an authoritative manner and in strikingly vivid, often highly metaphorical language.

Hooker constantly taught the importance of introspection, meditation, and self-examination. It is by looking inward that man will discover not only his viciously sinful nature but also the germs of God's saving grace. Thus in *The Christians Two Chiefe Lessons, Viz. Selfe-Deniall and Selfe-Tryal,* Hooker used as a text II Corinthians 13:5: "Examine yourselves whether ye be in the faith; prove yourselves." He argued that just as men seek security in worldly things, so they should be "hot and eager" to get assurance of salvation, which can come only from examining one's heart. One of the main purposes of life, according to Hooker, is to gain this assurance; therefore, one should regularly set aside some time for self-examination. The heart of man is full of "infinite windings and secret turnings" that make the process complex and time-consuming, and there are times when one cannot determine his spiritual state, but this fact, argued Hooker, should not discourage self-examination.[3]

Hooker's characteristic Puritan theology assumed predestination, but he is thoroughly practical, not theoretical, and his teachings are set forth in language that is both direct and dignified. Frequently his imagery is dramatic, full of personalities and conflicts. Even Hooker's God has a personality, or rather three, since Hooker emphasized the Trinity. Before God made man, "the three Persons enter into a consultation to set upon this masterpiece." Then they conversed, explained Hooker: " 'I will create,' saith the Father, 'and do you create, Son, and do you create, Spirit.' " Hooker's God the Father has a split personality: He is all justice and all mercy. The Son is pictured as having a tender heart for sinners. Hooker's interest is in the Son and the risen Christ, not Jesus, in the Son who performed theological functions.[4]

The man that the Trinity created had access to spiritual knowledge that he lost with the Fall. Originally, his mental faculties functioned perfectly. Reason and holiness commanded both the understanding and the affections so well that man could will what was right. Thus before the Fall, man was, nevertheless, free to choose either good or evil with equal ease. But man sinned and lost his liberty with the Fall. With him all men lost their liberty, for Adam "represented all mankind. He stood (as a Parliament man doth for the whole country) for all that should be born of him, so that look what Adam did, all his posterity did." All men may be justly condemned for Adam's sin, "though they never commit actual sin." Thus "if we had dropped out of our mother's womb into Hell and there been roaring, . . . it had been just."[5]

The man that God has now to deal with is natural man, fallen man, and God's task in dealing with man is complicated by the peculiar psychological functioning of this man. His nature now lacks any holiness or righteousness. His understanding functions so poorly that he makes many mistakes. He "walks in darkness or at most by the starlight of reason." He does retain some knowledge of what is right, so that he has a conscience. Since, however, the will may not choose to accept what the understanding proposes, he may be willingly ignorant. Thus when the understanding is able to provide a truth, man may refuse it as too hard for him to bear. Competing with the understanding are "delight and desire," and they "outbid reason." Thus man inevitably sins. The means by which he can escape from sin, grace, is not available to him: he is "not capable of grace and is unwilling to be made capable."[6]

God punished Adam and all mankind for the Fall with sin and death. The scheme of redemption that was arranged was, however, virtually a necessity, for, without it, God's purpose in creating the world would have been frustrated, his mercy not manifested, and "the elect fallen without this would have had no comfort." Therefore in conference the Trinity arrived at a plan. The Son agreed to put himself "into the room of a sinner." God then proceeded against him with the Law of God so that justice would be done. The Son as Christ suffered death, but only for the elect, for had he died for everyone, God's justice would have received two payments for the sins of the damned, Christ's death and their own punishments. (Hooker assumed an acceptance on the part of his audience of the concepts of election and reprobation.) Christ died for the elect, or more specifically atoned for the sins of the elect, whom Hooker called "the believers" since the salvation of the elect comes by faith. Then comes the next step in the redemption process, justification. "The debts and sins of the believer are charged upon the Lord Jesus Christ, and by the merits and satisfaction of Christ [are] imputed to the believer; he is accounted just and so is acquitted before God as righteous." In this scheme the act of justification is the Father's, since He was the person offended by Adam's sin. God the Father now becomes the creditor, the Son is the surety, and the Holy Ghost the messenger who brings the notice of acquittance. After a man has been justified, the benefits that are now his must be made effective to him through vocation or effectual calling. The decree of justification is the means by which the elect receive the benefit of the atonement, from the divine point of view; from the human point of view faith is the means. The elect are called and given the necessary · faith, an operation that Hooker describes picturesquely: "When the Father hath revealed that so many in such a place shall be saved, the Lord Christ undertakes the care of them, and he calls at such a door, and saith, I must have the poor drunken creature, and he must be humbled and broken hearted, and he must believe."[7]

More specifically, Hooker describes vocation as having two steps. First, "the Lord draws the sinner from himself and his corruptions and breaks that cursed league and combination that is between sin and the soul." Second, the soul is made "to lie upon and to close with the Lord Jesus Christ." God develops this new relationship, saving faith, by recognizing that the fallen-but-elected man whom He is to call is a creature of desires. He therefore takes advantage of man's selfish nature by offering Christ as a desirable gift that will preserve and help man. God appeals to all of a man's faculties: to the understanding, the affections, and the will. Not until the mind understands what faith is and until the affections and the will long for it does God send it. God's appealing to the mind is a necessary preparation for salvation, for without it redemption would appear unreasonable. But it is even more important that the will, "the great commander of the soul," be prepared, for the intellectual process of believing is not enough.[8]

Two of Hooker's descriptions of God's techniques, both vividly dramatic, show how he thought vocation was effected:

Many a saint can say that the Lord had been wrestling with him from the time of his childhood, and all along in the places where he lived [there were] strange horrors and then strange humiliation and abasement for this. Grace is not yet wrought, that's true, but it's working. The sovereign virtue of the blood of Christ is now at work and will never leave the soul for which Christ died until there be a full and effectual application of all saving good.

In the same work, Hooker explains that God first lets the soul see that it is not in the way to salvation, then it lets it see his mercy, and Christ's sufficiency. If these do not convert the soul, and Hooker implies that they cannot be expected to do so, then God stirs up the conscience. But Satan fights back:

The world by her allurements, Satan by his temptations and the accursed delights of our sinful lusts, they all besiege the soul, and by their wiles persuade the sinner to join sides with them, and not to be awed or carried away by the contrary command. "These be," say they, "threatenings announced, but threatened men live long. This wind shakes no corn. This is no way of policy to scare men, but it is not in earnest to hurt men. The same has been spoken to others, but nothing inflicted upon them. They never found, never felt, any such blows as all these terrible shakings of the rod pretend." Thus the sinner is yet drawn aside to follow his sinful courses. Conscience therefore makes after him, lays violent hands upon him, and holds him faster than ever. He becomes an accuser of him who was only a friendly admonisher before.

The soul is then called back to its sinful courses yet another time, and, as a result, God declares, "Let him perish in his sins, for he rejected mercy." The soul now sees its position clearly. Then, and only then, God plucks him out of his sin and calls him to sainthood.[9]

According to these descriptions, God is an expert psychologist,

and effectual calling is effectual, seemingly, because of the nicety of
the divine timing. Should one ask how God can announce that He
will permit the mercy-rejecting sinner to perish, only to call him
effectually later, the answer seems to be that Hooker's account of
vocation is man's view of the process: God chooses to make His
grace appear to be resistible rather than to rape man's will and understanding.

As a result of justification and vocation, man is adopted and the
process of sanctification begins. Now man works from the power of
grace. Every faculty of the soul is touched, and there are "wisdom
and prudence in the mind, holiness in the will, harmonious
readiness in all the affections." Man does not become perfect, and
he must ask for grace to resist temptation and avoid sin. There is
nevertheless progress till death.[10]

In this summary nothing has been said about the preacher,
though in fact the whole process happens by means of the sermon:
"The work of the Spirit doth always go with and is accompanied by
the Word." This is not to say that every sermon is used by God to
communicate saving grace to every hearer: "The same dispensation
of the Word which is powerful and profitable to some is un-
profitable to others." This concept deserves examination. A good
beginning is provided by a comment, a commonplace one, from a
Hooker sermon: "What a thing is this, then, when neither minister
can persuade thee, nor angels exhort thee, nor Christ himself entreat thee to take mercy?" Is Hooker saying that men can resist
God? No, for as a Calvinist he believed that grace was irresistible.
Or is he saying that persuasion ought to be enough to call a man to
salvation? No, for more than mere persuasion is necessary. The
answer is that neither was meant. Hooker's technique was to use
persuasion, the strongest persuasion he could, with the thought that
if anyone responded, it was because God gave him the ability to respond, gave him the heart to respond. Man needs something to
which he can respond, and the sermon is the Lord's instrument.
When Hooker urges his hearers to "bestir our souls in the use of all
means to entertain a saviour" and then promises that, if they do,
"we shall not miss of our expectation," he knows that only the elect
will choose to "use the means" (to follow the preacher's directions),
and "without means thou hast no reason to think that God will
work." If men have "prayers and sermons and exhortations and ad-
monitions and comforts," then they have "all things that are
available to bring a man to life and happiness," for these means, "so

far as He is pleased to appoint and use them," are instrumental causes of the application of redemption to sinners. The last phrase quoted is always understood, if not always so clearly stated.[11]

While Hooker's technique of persuasion is both subtle and powerful, what is most striking about it is the difficulty that he anticipates in the salvation of any sinner. In later life he seems to have thought the difficulty even greater than he had when he preached his earlier sermons. Thus in the tenth book of *The Application of Redemption*, a treatise on contrition, he explains that true contrition

will cost much labor and long time, before it can be done in an ordinary way; and therefore if thou art wise for thy soul omit no time, be faithful to do what thou canst, and yet fearful, because it's in God's hands to do what He will. Therefore seek seasonably, tremblingly, and uncessantly unto the Lord to do this work for thee. It's not the dipping but rubbing and soaking of an old stain that will fetch it out. Thou must soak and steep thy soul with godly sorrow. It's not salving but long tenting an old sore that will do the cure. It may make you go crying to your grave, and well if you get to heaven at last.

Hooker encourages his hearers not to procrastinate for even if the process is slow, it must be begun.[12]

As a preacher eager to persuade his hearers to use the means of salvation, Hooker was much interested in setting forth the rewards the saints will receive. Since, like most American Puritans, Hooker chose not to dwell on the quality of the life after death, the joys of salvation that he describes are nearly always to be achieved in this life. First of these always is assurance of salvation. Other joys are often strangely intangible: "all spiritual good," "unconceivable good," "unsearchable riches." Sometimes the description of the joys to be gained is highly metaphorical: "God will come and sup with them that follow him." Hooker's technique in describing the life of those who have been called is strikingly similar to his description of conversion. For the unconverted, conversion is depicted as the ultimate goal, but for the converted, nothing is really settled. One must continually test his conversion. And Hooker provides very full descriptions concerning how this exhausting task should be undertaken. The search for assurance that one had been saved sometimes led to a substitution of assurance for salvation itself. Men were to descend into themselves in their religious search, not reach up to God.[13]

Besides these psychological techniques, Hooker used in his sermons a whole arsenal of literary techniques. He spiced his sermons with personifications, bits of imagined conversations between virtues and vices, the devil, Christ, God, the soul, mercy, justice; many appeals to the senses; imagery drawn from gardening, housekeeping, law, and medicine; rough colloquialisms; proverbs, parallelisms, antitheses, alliteration, repetition. Perhaps Hooker's most effective technique is his use of characters: descriptions of types of people, particularly types of the unconverted. He thus describes a sinner who will not confess:

He must be drawn like a bear to make open confession as the cause may require, and when he comes by constraint, conscience drags him, or authority compels him thereunto. His acknowledgements stick in his teeth. He lisps them out so wearishly, hacks and hewes, stops here and there, as though he would say something because he must speak, and yet he is afraid he shall say more than he would, therefore bites in his words one way, sometimes turns his speech another way. If any speech seems too open, or to give too much advantage to the truth, he recalls himself and begins to qualify what he hath said, i.e., his meaning is to conceal as much as he can.[14]

Two dominant features of American Puritanism appear in Thomas Hooker's eloquent sermons. His preaching encouraged the individual to cultivate what is within and to separate himself from his fellows. Giving priority to one's private, inner life, an inner-directedness, a psychological remoteness from one's fellows—these became consequences of the New England Puritan tradition. Another closely related quality has been given a name: the New England conscience. One who is encouraged to look within for assurance of salvation—but is warned that he may not find it—may create a very high moral standard for himself. The conscience-ridden Puritan as seen in, say, Hawthorne's Dimmesdale of *The Scarlet Letter* was not a creation of the imagination, as the diaries of such Puritans as Michael Wigglesworth show.

II *The Founding of Harvard College*

Harvard College received special attention in *New Englands First Fruits*, and well it might, for the creation of an institution of higher learning within the first decade was probably New England's most remarkable accomplishment. It was, Cotton Mather explained at the end of the century, "the best thing that ever New England thought upon." The creation of Harvard was the result of many factors, first and foremost of which was the Puritans' devotion to learning. A very high percentage of immigrants were university men—a high percentage, that is, in a day when university education was a relative rarity. In 1640, according to one count, there were 113 university men in New England, seventy-one of whom were in the Massachusetts Bay colony.[15]

While some of these men were laymen (such as John Winthrop, who had studied for a year or two at Trinity College, Cambridge), most were ministers. Since many of these had been attracted to Puritanism while students, they associated the ministry with learning, as the *First Fruits* demonstrates: "After God had carried us safe to New England, and we had builded our houses, provided necessaries for our livelihood, reared convenient places for God's worship, and settled the civil government, one of the next things we longed after was to advance learning and perpetuate it to our posterity, dreading to leave an illiterate ministry to the churches, when our present ministers shall lie in the dust."[16]

The creation of Harvard was the act of the General Court of Massachusetts Bay, which agreed in 1636 to provide eight hundred pounds for "a school or college" over the next several years. This sum amounted to half of the tax levy for the entire colony in 1636. Somewhat later the Court decided that "the college is ordered to be at Newetown," and then changed the name of that town to Cambridge, as a way of identifying the college town with the great university back in Old England. The site seems to have been chosen because the town had remained untouched by Hutchinsonian doctrine during the Antinomian controversy. Thomas Shepard's ministry was considered worthy protection there, and, as Edward Johnson observed, "spiritual learning was the thing they chiefly desired."[17]

Harvard was modeled after Emmanuel College, Cambridge, which had been founded "to render as many as possible fit for the administration of the divine word and sacraments." Shepard had been a student there, as had John Cotton, Thomas Hooker, and the famous Massachusetts schoolmaster, Ezekiel Cheever. In all, some fifteen Emmanuel men were in New England in the early years. The least important, perhaps, in every way but one was John Harvard, who came to New England in 1637, much later than most of the others. Then twenty-nine, he had settled in Charlestown, where he performed some ministerial functions before he died in 1638. He left the college 850 pounds, though it may not have received all the money due it. He also left the college his library of four hundred volumes. In recognition, the Court called the college Harvard.[18]

Classes began in 1638, with nine students, but only a year later the college ceased operation because Harvard's first master, Nathaniel Eaton, was discharged as "cruel and barbarous." Henry Dunster, made President in 1640 at the age of thirty, remained in office for fourteen years and was a most successful leader. A graduate of Magdalene College, Cambridge, he had been a schoolmaster and clergyman. His speciality was Hebrew.[19]

Admission to Harvard was chiefly conditioned on an ability to read Cicero "or such like Latin author *extempore* and make and speak true Latin in verse and prose . . . and decline perfectly the paradigm of nouns and verbs in the Greek tongue. . . ." Students admitted were closely supervised, for education at Harvard meant not merely academic education but education in piety. While only about one half of Harvard's graduates in the seventeenth century entered the ministry, in its first twenty years of existence it produced one hundred and eleven ministers, a number that more than met the needs of New England. Some graduates took up ministries in England and Ireland. The continuation of the Puritan ministry justified the college's existence in the view of the leaders of New England.[20]

The early Harvard curriculum featured heavy emphasis on languages. Students continued their reading of Greek each year, and in their first year began the study of Hebrew. These languages were given extensive attention. Rather less was devoted to Aramaic and Syriac, both being studied for one year. The curriculum also included lectures, always in Latin, in mathematics and astronomy, logic, physics, politics, rhetoric, history and geography, and the nature of plants. Much time was devoted to philosophy, to Aristotelian metaphysics and ethics. The second president of Harvard felt obligated in 1655 to defend such studies in a Christian education. He justified them on the grounds that the Bible itself treats natural philosophy and "ethical, political and moral precepts" and that in the Bible are to be found "all sorts of rhetorical tropes and figures" as well as "the best and surest chronology in the world." At the end of the century, President Increase Mather quoted and amplified a saying of Aristotle: "Find a friend in Plato, a friend in Socrates (and I say a friend in Aristotle), but above all find a friend in TRUTH."[21]

Each Saturday Harvard students focused on catechetical divinity, with William Ames's *Medulla* or *Marrow of Sacred Theology* the text. Students were expected to know the Bible well and to be able to analyze it logically—to derive syllogisms from Biblical texts. More advanced studies of divinity were post-baccalaureate. Some graduates remained in Cambridge; others began their ministerial careers immediately. In either instance, they were expected to continue their studies independently. Their readings were now much more strictly theological. They read the Church Fathers; the Scholastics; the great Biblical commentators; the Reformed theologians such as Calvin, Peter Martyr, William Perkins, Zanchius. The library of Harvard graduate Edward Taylor is suggestive. It included Foxe's *Acts and Monuments*, the writings of Saint Augustine, Calvin's *Institutes* and two volumes of his sermons, Cartwright's harmony of the Gospels, two of John Cotton's works, Ames's *De Conscientia*. About a third of his library was in Latin.[22]

Old Cambridge was a lively intellectual center, where rival philosophies had to compete. New Cambridge was a small provincial town, where indoctrination was provided. Some Harvard men did visit the mother country for a time before taking up ministerial tasks in New England. Increase Mather, for instance, spent four years in various preaching posts in England and in Ireland, where he studied at Trinity College, Dublin, which awarded him an M.A. The existence of Harvard permitted New England to remain intellectually independent of England, and while it created provincialism, it permitted the continuation of the Puritan tradition, which was dying in the place of its origin. Harvard could not be expected to produce adequate replacements for the founders, who had been self-selected volunteers for the New England experience.[23]

III *Puritans and Poetry*

New England's traditional preeminence in literature was not greatly encouraged by Harvard. Rhetoric and metaphorical analysis were parts of the curriculum, and some students developed a taste for Greek and Latin verse and drama. But whether or not Harvard was responsible, a great deal of verse was written in early New England. Poetry of merit continues to turn up, including poems of the greatest poet of colonial America, Edward Taylor. Much too much has been said about Puritan antagonism to literature. There has been a failure to distinguish, as the Puritans did, between literature as popular amusement and literature as art. While the Puritans usually rejected the love lyric and the theater, they respected and admired other forms of writing, including poetry.[24]

Poetry was expected to be serious, but not necessarily solemn. Wit was a very common ingredient of verse, even in elegies, poems that celebrated the dead and the ideals of the founders. Members of the second generation, feeling a deep sense of loss as the fathers of New England passed on, celebrated the founders in verse. One of the best as well as most typical of early New England elegies is Urian Oakes's "An Elegie upon the Death of the Reverend Thomas Shepard," actually Thomas Shepard Junior, who died in 1677. Its author, a learned man, served briefly as president of Harvard. The "Elegie" is a jeremiad: Oakes sees New England as a covenanted community that may soon suffer sorely for its sins, now more likely to be visited by God's wrath, since Shepard was, according to Oakes, a creator of harmony, a mediator between God and the community. Oakes attempts to make his poem serve a purpose similar to that performed by Shepard's ministry, to reawaken the community to its collective responsibility to God.

The original is 342 lines. Here are some of its verses:

> Dear Shepard, could we reach so high a strain
> Of pure seraphic love, as to divest
> Ourselves, and love, of self-respect, thy gain
> Would joy us, though it cross our interest.
>   Then would we silence all complaints with this,
>   Our dearest friend is doubtless gone to bliss.

> As when some formidable comets blaze,
> As when portentous prodigies appear,
> Poor mortals with amazement stand and gaze,
> With hearts affrighted, and with trembling fear:
>   So are we all amazed at this blow,
>   Sadly portending some approaching woe.

> Learned he was beyond the common size,
> Befriended much by nature in his wit
> And temper (sweet, sedate, ingenious, wise)
> And (which crown'd all) he was Heav'n's favorite:
>   Or whom the God of all grace did command,
>   And show'r down blessings with a liberal hand.

See what our sins have done! What ruins wrought:
And how they have pluck'd out our very eyes!
Our sins have slain our Shepard! we have bought
And dearly paid for, our enormities.
  Ah cursed sins! that strike at God, and kill
  His servants, and the blood of prophets spill.

New-England! know thy heart-plague: feel this blow;
A blow that sorely wounds both head and heart,
A blow that reaches all, both high and low,
A blow that may be felt in every part.
  Mourn that this great man's fall'n in Israel:
  Lest it be said, with him New-England fell!

Oakes ends his poem by calling Shepard his "dearest, inmost bosom-friend," but the occasion of the poem is less important than Oakes's contemplation of Puritan virtue. Through his poem he seeks to stir up his fellow Puritans to greater piety and stricter morality.[25]

IV   *Anne Bradstreet: The Tenth Muse*

Two Puritan poets have survived the test of time as more than historical curiosities: Anne Bradstreet and Edward Taylor. Both were unusual. Bradstreet is the first significant woman poet writing in English, and Edward Taylor is the last poet to write in the metaphysical tradition created by George Chapman and John Donne. Each had a distinctive poetic personality that has been much discussed. A good deal about New England Puritanism can be learned from their poetry.[26]

Born in 1613 as Anne Dudley, New England's first real poet spent much of her early life in Lincolnshire, where her father, Thomas, was steward for the Puritan Earl of Lincoln. Through the encouragement of her father, she became well educated, well read in history and literature. At the age of about fifteen, she married Simon Bradstreet, ten years her senior and a graduate of Emmanuel College, Cambridge. In 1630 she came to America with her father, mother, husband, and her brothers and sisters. They settled at Newetown, later Cambridge. (Her father was serving as lieutenant governor of the colony). Later she lived at Ipswich, where the whole Dudley-Bradstreet clan moved within a few years. Then in 1645, the Bradstreets moved to the new settlement of North Andover, where Anne lived until her death in 1672.[27]

Anne Bradstreet had a baby soon after she arrived in America and eventually produced eight children. Soon after her arrival she also began to write poetry and eventually composed a substantial quantity. During her first twenty years in America she worked with care at her craft and polished her art, though she produced little poetry of consequence. As a woman, she was made to feel defensive about her poetry:

> I am obnoxious to each carping tongue
> Who says my hand a needle better fits,
> A poet's pen all scorn I should thus wrong,
> For such despite they cast on female wits:
> If what I do prove well, it won't advance;
> They'll say it's stol'n, or else it was by chance.

In 1650, without her permission, a volume of her poems was published in London, *The Tenth Muse Lately sprung up in America*. The poems were "By a Gentlewoman of those parts," the title page explained. After her death, an enlarged volume appeared, published in Boston in 1678: *Several Poems Compiled with great variety of Wit and Learning, Full of Delight.* John Woodbridge, who prepared an epistle to the reader, noted defensively that the poems are "the fruit but of some few hours, curtailed from her sleep and other refreshments." The new poems, and some others published in the nineteenth century, are the ones most likely to interest modern readers.[28]

At its best, Anne Bradstreet's poetry dramatizes what was perhaps the central Puritan problem: how to live in the world without becoming worldly. Puritan preachers seldom paid much attention to the world to come; they tried to explain how to live in the present world. Anne Bradstreet wrote on "The Vanity of All Worldly Things" but also celebrated her love for her husband:

> If ever two were one, then surely we.
> If ever man were loved by wife, then thee;
> If ever wife were happy in a man,
> Compare with me, ye women, if you can.

She faced the problem of "The Flesh and the Spirit" in a poem with that title, but without a full recognition of the former's claims. In one of her seventy-seven "Meditations Divine and Moral" she describes more emphatically the appeals of the world: "Some children are hardly weaned. Although the teat be rubbed with wormwood or mustard, they will either wipe it off or else suck down sweet and bitter together. So it is with some Christians. Let God embitter all the sweets of this life, that so they might feed upon more substantial food, yet they are so childishly sottish that they are still hugging and sucking these empty breasts that God is forced to hedge up their way with thorns or lay affliction on their loins that so they might shake hands with the world before it bid them farewell." Anne Bradstreet knew the sweets of this life. She knew, as a New Englander, of the delights of spring: "After a long winter we see the leafless trees and dry stocks at the approach of the sun to resume their former vigor and beauty in a more ample manner than what they lost in the autumn." But for her spring was also "a lively emblem of the resurrection."[29]

In her long meditative poem "Contemplations" Anne Bradstreet emphasized the opposing appeals of this world, the world of nature, and the next world, the world of God. The poem is said to strike notes of Keats, Shelley, Wordsworth, even Shakespeare. But it is also very much Anne Bradstreet's own poem. Here she writes of how the riches of the autumnal scene, its "delectable view," "rapt" her senses. But she is soon led to recognize that "If so much excellence abide below,/How excellent is he that dwells on high?" Each aspect of nature that grasps her attention receives adequate recognition, even celebration, and as her attention moves from nature to the supernatural she does not choose to dismiss the former altogether. Nor does she preach the Wordsworthian gospel of nature. She constantly finds nature edifying, leading her to a deeper understanding of God, as she reads nature allegorically. Perhaps because as a Puritan she was suspicious of private revelation, Bradstreet often grounds the relationship that she sees between object and God as authority stronger than individual private perception. Nature gives her a new awareness of the Bible's teachings.[30]

If nature's glories lead her to a rediscovery of God's glory, if (for instance) the sun leads her to God because they resemble one another, she found only what the Psalmist found:

> Then higher on the glistening sun I gazed,
> Whose beams were shaded by the leavie tree;
> The more I looked, the more I grew amazed,
> And softly said, "What glory's like to thee?"

. . . .

Thou as a bridegroom from thy chamber rushes,
And as a strong man joys to run a race;
The morn doth usher thee with smiles and blushes;
The earth reflects her glances in thy face;

. . . .

Art thou so full of glory that no eye
Hath strength thy shining rays once to behold?
And is thy splendid throne erect so high,
As to approach it, can no earthly mould?
How full of glory then may thy Creator be,
Who gave this bright light luster unto thee?
Admired, adored forever, be that majesty.

The poet is, however, not satisfied with the concept that nature
serves as a symbol of God, for she—as human—perceives herself to
be omitted from the relationship. Man is isolated from nature.

Silent, alone, where none or saw or heard,
In pathless paths I led by wand'ring feet,
My humble eyes to lofty skies I reared
To sing some song, my mazed Muse thought meet.
My great Creator I would magnify,
That nature had thus decked liberally;
But Ah, and Ah, again, my imbecility!
I heard the merry grasshopper then sing,
The black-clad cricket bear a second part;
They kept one tune and played on the same string,
Seeming to glory in their little art.
Shall creatures abject thus their voices raise,
And in their kind resound their Maker's praise,
Whilst I, as mute, can warble forth no higher lays?

Her recognition of the intimate relationship between nature and
God leaves her only with a sense of her own inadequacy, her own
limitations.

Turning away from nature for relief from her sense of loneliness
and isolation, she next contemplates Biblical history. She sees there
Adam's sin; she sees Cain and Abel. She imagines Adam sighing

> . . . to see his progeny
> Clothed all in his black sinful livery
> Who neither guilt nor yet the punishment could fly.

Both in history and in nature she sees the hand of God. But she finds no personal consolation in either. For nature, unlike man, continues its endless cycles of the seasons with each spring bringing rebirth; for history shows all of humanity, each individual who has lived on the earth, ultimately captured by "perpetual night":

> When I behold the heavens as in their prime,
> And then the earth (though old) still clad in green,
> The stones and trees, insensible of time,
> Nor age nor wrinkle on their front are seen:
> If winter come and greenness then do fade,
> A spring returns, and they more youthful made;
> But man grows old, lies down, remains where once he's laid.

Finding no comfort for herself in either nature or history, the poet can turn only to faith, to a conviction that man is happily not caught up in the cycles of nature but rather was "made for endless immortality." Man differs from nature too in that he is subject to moral judgment. Even if human history is a history of depravity, even if life inevitably leads to death, death offers the promise of life, not merely the recycling of nature, but a new and better life beyond the grave.

With a new sense of her relationship to the universe, the poet looks at nature again. She who saw aspects of nature as emblems of God now sees a river, and the river becomes for her "emblem true" of MAN.

> "Oh happy flood," quoth I, "that holds thy race
> Till thou arrive at thy beloved place
> Nor is it rocks or shoals that can obstruct thy pace."

The river's movement to its destination resembles the movement of the saved soul to God. Nature, she finds, may help her to see herself in her relationship to God.

According to "Contemplations," nature can serve as an emblem of both God and man. It can be useful as a means of achieving a heightened awareness of God's truth and of man's position in the universe. But it is not to be relied upon, not to be trusted in:

The mariner that on smooth waves doth glide
Sings merrily and steers his bark with ease,
As if he had command of wind and tide,
And now become great master of the seas:
But suddenly a storm spoils all the sport,
And makes him long for a more quiet port,
Which 'gainst all adverse winds may serve for fort.

"Contemplations" is a poem about man's struggles with himself, with the human condition, in which one directly faces nature, not God, in daily life. How to avoid taking "this earth ev'n for heaven's bower," how to perceive rightly man's place in God's universe and in providential history, is the burden of Anne Bradstreet's poem. The structure of the poem is not always satisfactory, and at times the poet resorts to clichés or hastens on too quickly to convictions that one senses she held in reserve to turn to. But nonetheless the poem is a serious one, on an important subject, important especially for an understanding of how a Puritan might think about man, God, history, and nature.

All of Anne Bradstreet's poetry is not reflective of the Puritanism that is strikingly evident in her prose. But those who see Puritanism as a force in opposition to literary creativity must contend with the fact that some of Bradstreet's best poetry, especially in "Contemplations," is Puritan in outlook.

V   Edward Taylor: Poet of Passionate Wit

As to Edward Taylor's Puritanism, there are now no arguments. When his poetry was first discovered, in the 1930s and 1940s, some critics unsympathetic with Puritanism related it to the Catholic tradition (how Taylor would have resented that!), or they called it heterodox, or they argued for the influence of Cambridge Platonism. More recently, the case for Taylor as a staunch Puritan has been well established.[31]

Edward Taylor, born in England in 1642, came to America in 1668, after the reconstitution of episcopacy with the Church of England and the restoration of monarchy. He had received something of an education at a dissenting (Puritan) academy, and had served as a schoolmaster. He attended Harvard as an advanced student, and there he became friendly with several future Puritan leaders, notably Increase Mather and Samuel Sewall. He enjoyed Harvard immensely, for he was a very bookish person. In 1671 he was graduated, but before he left Harvard, he began a library by copying by hand books that he was too poor to buy. This practice, which he continued throughout his life, is an indication of his devotion to learning. He left Cambridge to serve as minister at Westfield, Massachusetts, and he did not return to take his master of arts degree until 1720, when he was seventy-eight.[32]

Westfield, west of the Connecticut River and not far north of Connecticut, was a frontier community. Taylor settled there, though for reasons not clear he did not organize a church until 1679. In this village, where he remained all his life, Taylor served as physician, peacemaker, disciplinarian, and preacher. Church records and surviving sermons show him to have been an active, effective leader and a widely read one. A surviving love letter to the woman he was to marry shows that he combined passion and theology in courtship as well as in preaching and in the composition of poetry. Of his love, he writes,

> Look not (I entreat you) on it as one of Love's hyperboles. If I borrow the beams of some sparkling metaphor to illustrate my respects unto thyself by, for your having made my breast a cabinet of your affections (as I yours mine), I know not how to offer a fitter comparison to set out my love by, than to compare it to a golden ball of pure fire rolling up and down my breast, from which there flies now and then a spark like a glorious beam from the body of the flaming sun. . . . My dear love, lest my letter should be judged the layish language of a lover's pen, I shall endeavor to show that conjugal love ought to exceed all other love. . . . But yet it must be kept within bounds too. For it must be subordinate to God's glory. The wish that mine may be so, it having got you into my heart, doth offer my heart with you in it as a more rich sacrifice unto God through Christ. . . .

What he had said in prose he later said rather better in verse. When his first wife died at the age of thirty-nine, soon after the birth of their eighth child, Taylor wrote:

> Some deem death doth the true love knot untie,
> But I do find it harder tied thereby.
> My heart is in't and will be squeez'd therefore
> To pieces if thou draw the ends much more.
> Oh strange untying! it ti'th harder. What?
> Can anything untie a true love knot?
> Five babes thou tookst from me before this stroke.
> Thine arrows then into my bowels broke,
> But now they pierce into my bosom smart,

> Do strike and stob me in the very heart.
> I'd then my bosom friend, a comfort, and
> To comfort. Yet, my Lord, I kiss thy hand.
> I her resign'd; thou tookst her into thine;
> Out of my bosom, yet she dwells in mine.

He married again, and in all he fathered fourteen children. Each of his surviving six daughters married a minister, and one of his two sons became a minister. He contributed much to the Puritan tradition.[33]

Taylor served as minister till 1725, when he was eighty-three, and he lived on until 1729. Throughout his life he composed poetry, some even before he came to America. His total output is over forty thousand lines, more than twice that of John Milton. In 1682, at the age of forty, he began a major poetic undertaking—an act of devotion as well: the composition of two long series of Preparatory Meditations. The full title of the poems, as he himself labeled it, is "Preparatory Meditations before my Approach to the Lords Supper. Chiefly upon the Doctrin preached upon the Day of administration." The better than two hundred poems that he wrote over the years up to 1725 are a singular achievement. Yet Taylor neither published nor prepared any of these poems for publication, the complete texts of which did not appear until 1960. Yet for Taylor the poems served a purpose: for him as for other orthodox Puritans the Lord's Supper was for the regenerate, and careful prior self-examination was necessary to determine whether one could faithfully receive it.[34]

Each meditation is based on a Biblical text or on a doctrine derived from the text, and the imagery of each poem is heavily dependent on suggestions in the Biblical text. In preparing his imaginative, witty, passionate and pious poetry Taylor was profoundly influenced by the metaphysical poetic tradition of George Herbert, Richard Crashaw, and John Cleveland. (Other Puritans wrote in this tradition as well: John Fiske, for example.) The tradition encouraged the yoking of wit and passion; it recognized the value of the pun; it authorized fantastic imagery, and Taylor himself wrote double and quadruple acrostics. "Wilderness baroque" is a term that has been used to describe Taylor's poetry, and the term fits. His "earthly enjoyment of things divine," as the same critic has put it, makes his technique exactly right for what he is trying to express. Taylor describes with relish the food and drink of the Lord's Supper as "Heaven's sugar-cake," as "roast mutton," as "aqua vitae." His excitement, his ecstasy drives him to radical metaphor:

> Of God: "Who in this bowling alley bowled the sun?"
> Of himself: "My members dung carts that bedung at pleasure."
> Of salvation: "Man marry God? God be a match for mud?"

Because he was a passionate man with a great gift for the fresh phrase, Taylor does not fit one's conception of the Puritan. The satisfactions that Taylor found in his religion are, however, not necessarily different from what other Puritans felt. Taylor's feelings as he prepares for the receiving of the Lord's Supper resemble closely Thomas Shepard's, for example, and Puritans commonly compared the believer's union with God to marriage.[35]

Let us examine two of Taylor's meditations that may serve as samples of his art and his thought. Meditation 60 B of the Second Series has as its text I Corinthians 10:4: "And did all drink the same spiritual drink." St. Paul is here referring to the exodus of the Israelites from Egypt, when according to Paul "they drank of that spiritual rock that followed them, and that rock was Christ." For Taylor, the reference is clearly to the Lord's Supper, where Christ's blood is drunk; the rock of Horeb (Exodus 17:6) is a foreshadowing or type of Christ's institution of the Supper, where the blood that Christ sacrificed on the cross is made available as atonement for the sins of the faithful. Seeing that a relationship can be developed between Moses's striking the rock and the sacrament, Taylor wrote his poem around that imagery.[36]

The poem begins, as Taylor's customarily do, with the poet's plight:

> Ye angels bright, pluck from your wings a quill.
>   Make me a pen thereof that best will write.
> Lend me your fancy and angelic skill
>   To treat this theme, more rich than rubies bright.
>   My muddy ink and cloudy fancy dark
>   Will dull its glory, lacking highest art.

Taylor judges that the celebration of the Lord's greatness in feeding his people can best be undertaken from a human point of view, and he writes:

An eye at center righter may describe
The world's circumferential glory vast
As in its nut shell bed it snugs fast tied
Than any angel's pen can glory cast
Upon this drink drawn from the rock, tapt by
The rod of God, in Horeb, typicly.

Next Taylor undertakes to describe the glories of the spiritual drink. Here the poet becomes highly imaginative, as his language reflects his learning, his wit, his pleasure in sound, and his ecstasy:

Sea water strain'd through minerals, rocks, and sands,
    Well clarifi'd by sunbeams, dulcifi'd,
Insipid, sordid, swill, dishwater stands.
    But here's a rock of aqua-vitae tried.
    When once God broach'd it, out a river came
    To bath and bibble in, for Israel's train.

Some rocks have sweat. Some pillars bled out tears.
    But here's a river in a rock up tunn'd,
Not of sea water nor of swill. It's beer.
    No nectar like it. Yet it once unbund,
    A river down out runs through ages all,
    A fountain op'd, to wash off sin and fall.

From this celebration of the purity of the drink, Taylor moves to a theological analysis of the functions of the Lord's Supper for the faithful.

Christ is this Horeb's rock; the streams that slide
    A river is of aqua vitae dear,
Yet costs us nothing, gushing from his side.
    Celestial wine our sinsunk souls to cheer.
    This rock and water, sacramental cup
    Are made, Lord's Supper wine for us to sup.

This rock's the grape that Zion's vineyard bore
    Which Moses' rod did smiting pound, and press
Until its blood, the brook of life, run o'er,
    All glorious grace and gracious righteousness.
    We in this brook must bathe, and with faith's quill
    Suck grace and life out of this rock our fill.

Finally Taylor returns to his own needs, to his imperfections as poet-celebrant of God's glory, and to his expectation of Christ's ability to aid him through the Supper.

> Lord, oint me with this petro oil. I'm sick.
> Make me drink water of the rock. I'm dry.
> Me in this fountain wash. My filth is thick.
> I'm faint; give aqua vitae or I die.
> If in this stream thou cleanse and cherish me,
> My heart thy hallelujas pipe shall be.

In this meditation, Taylor employs language with great imaginative freedom, as in his use of the word *fall*. "In Adam's fall,/ We sinned all," the *New England Primer* declared. For Taylor *fall* is the infection that the sinner wears, which can, however, be washed off by the unlimited river that flows out of the unbunged tun. The poet is a Puritan, but the Puritan, with God's grace, is also a poet, as the last stanza asserts.

Though Taylor may employ similar imagery in several poems, his variety is nonetheless great. A striking example is Meditation 29, Second Series, in which he uses I Peter 3:20 as his text: "While the ark was building." Peter wrote of man's disobedience that led to the flood and God's salvation of only a few. Taylor finds the world still flooded with sin:

> What shall I say, my Lord, with what begin?
> Immense profaneness wormholes e'ry part.
> The world is saddleback'd with loads of sin.
> Sin cracks the axletree of this great cart.

To punish the sin-heavy world, God uses nature as his rod:

> Floodgates of fiery vengeance open fly,
> And smoky clouds of wrath darken the sky.

Despite the violence of this imagery, Taylor is not satisfied that he has suggested adequately the extent of God's wrath. Through the strong sounds of his verse he recreates the strong sounds of nature's violence:

> The Fountains of the Deep up broken are.
> The cataracts of heaven do boil o'er
> With wallowing seas. Thunder and lightning's tare

> Spouts out of heaven, floods out from hell do roar,
> To overflow and drown'd the world all drown'd
> And overflown with sin that doth abound.

Searching for a rescue craft, Taylor remembers that Christ walked on the water and that the ark was a type of Christ, or to put it another way, Christ is an antitype of the ark, the realization of what had been anticipated by the Old Testament story of the ark:

> Oh! for an ark, an ark of gopher wood.
>   This flood's too stately to be rode upon
> By other boats, which are base, swilling tubs.
>   It gulps them up as gudgeons, and they're gone.
>   But thou, my Lord, dost antitype this ark,
>   And rod'st upon these waves that toss and bark.

Using a combination of theological and ship-building terms, Taylor now develops the metaphor of Christ as an ark!

> Thy human nature (oh choice timber rich)
>   Bituminated o're within and out
> With dressing of the Holy Spirit's pitch,
>   Propitiatory grace parg'd round about,
>   This ark will ride upon the flood and live,
>   Nor passage to a drop through chink holes give.
>
> This ark will swim upon the fiery flood;
>   All show'rs of fire the heavens rain on't will
> Slide off. Though Hell's and Heaven's spouts out stood
>   And meet upon't to crush't to shivers, still
>   It neither sinks, breaks, fires, nor leaky proves,
>   But lives upon them all and upward moves.

But it is Christ as his personal savior that is Taylor's deepest concern, and so the poet asks that Christ "ark" him:

> All that would not be drownded must be in't,
>   Be ark'd in Christ, or else the cursed rout
> Of crimson sins their cargo will them sink
>   And suffocate in Hell, because without.
>   Then ark me, Lord, thus in thyself that I
>   May dance upon these drownding waves with joy.

In the next stanza Taylor paints a vivid picture of the peace that reigned in Noah's ark and of the peace that reigns when Christ provides grace:

> Sweet ark, with concord sweeten'd, in thee feed
> The calf, and bear, lamb, lion, at one crib.
> Here rattlesnake and squirrel jar not, breed.
> The hawk and dove, the leopard and the kid
> Do live in peace, the child and cockatrice.
> As if red sin tantarrow'd in no vice.

As usual, Taylor's meditation ends with a petition for salvation and a promise of poetry:

> Take me, my Lord, into thy golden ark.
> Then when thy flood of fire shall come, I shall
> Though Hell spews streams of flames, and th' Heavens spark
> Out storms of burning coals, swim safe o'er all.
> I'll make thy curled flames my cittern's wire
> To toss my songs of praise rung on them, higher.

As in this poem, Taylor's verse is full of images of failure, often specifically poetic failure: his pen is "jagging," his lips are "padlock'd fast," and his rhymes are "ragged." Many of his poems emphasize depravity and sinfulness, so much that his vision of life has been called "excremental." Flatulence, defecation, and every form of filth are Taylor's vivid labels for man's sin. Here is how Meditation 26, Second Series, begins:

> Unclean, unclean, my Lord, undone, all vile,
> Yea, all defil'd. What shall thy servant do?
> Unfit for thee, not fit for holy soil,
> Nor for communion of saints below.
> A bag of botches, lump of loathsomeness,
> Defil'd by touch, by issue, lepros'd flesh.

Taylor draws on toilet imagery, images of the barnyard and the swamp and bodily disease as images of man's sin; he draws on flower and perfume images to describe God's grace. All the world's glory, the world's best, is "but like drops dropp'd in a close-stool pan" (I, 48). Grace is "honeysuckles," "sweet spike," "Sharon's rose," and "Herba Trinitatis" (II, 62). God washes man's filth with "holy soap, and niter, and rich lye" (I, 40). Christ is a physician who can cure the sick and can feed the starving with himself: "Here is a feast indeed! in ev'ry dish/A whole redeemer cook'd up bravely," "a mess of delicates made of his blood" (II, 108). Taylor's imagery is powerful and effective but also traditional, for Calvin and others had described sin and grace as Taylor does.[37].

The Biblicalness of Puritanism was no bane to Taylor. He especially reveled in the Song of Solomon: nearly seventy texts are drawn from this book, cited by Taylor as Canticles. Of his many gospel texts, half were drawn from the poetic Gospel of John. Taylor also favored the epistles, especially Corinthians and Colossians.

Taylor wrote a great deal: a metrical history of Christianity in over twenty thousand lines, elegies, occasional poems. Besides the meditations, one other poem stands out, "Gods Determinations touching his Elect: /and the Elects Combat in their Conversion, /and Coming up to God in Christ together with the Comfortable Effects thereof." An effort to justify the ways of God to men, especially sinners, "Gods Determinations" is a didactic poem, but on a much higher level than Michael Wigglesworth's *The Day of Doom*, with which it has been compared. Frequently dramatic in style, the poem especially celebrates the congregational concept of church fellowship:

> Christ's Spirit showers
> Down in his Word and sacraments
> Upon these flowers
> The clouds of Grace divine contents.
> Such things of wealthy blessings on them fall
> As make them sweetly thrive. Yet that's not all.

At the end of his poem Taylor composes a vivid picture of the elect church members riding to glory together in Christ's coach:

> In all their acts, public and private, nay
> And secret too, they praise impart.
> But in their acts divine and worship, they
> With hymns do offer up their heart.
> Thus in Christ's coach they sweetly sing
> As they to glory ride therein.

Puritan doctrine was Edward Taylor's poetic inspiration: man's depravity, God's glory, justice, and mercy, election and salvation, the Lord's Supper as a seal of salvation, violent anti-Catholicism too. Puritan doctrine was not something with which Taylor struggled in his poetry; he embraced it, with its demanding morality and its warm piety, its sense of the enormous gulf between God and man. It is difficult to imagine that Taylor would have become a serious, major poet without his commitment to Puritanism. Though often obscure, Taylor's poetry can help modern students of Puritanism to appreciate its appeal.

Few in number, busy with the tasks required for survival, the Puritans began in New England a culture that was to influence America profoundly. Some of the fruits of that culture are Thomas Hooker's sermons, the first American college, and two notable poets.

CHAPTER 6

Glimpses at the Puritan Consciousness

P URITAN doctrine—the theology of the catechism, the tract, and the sermon—served as guidelines for countless early New Englanders. From the cradle to the grave, Puritanism was omnipresent. *Milk for Babes*, John Cotton's catechism, went through nine editions in the seventeenth century, though it was only one of fourteen New England catechisms published. (Many American Puritans continued to use William Perkins's catechism.) Two services of preaching and Bible exposition were held every Sunday, and attendance was expected. According to *The Book of the General Lawes and Libertyes Concerning the Inhabitants of the Massachusetts* (1648), since "the ministry of the word is established according to the order of the Gospel throughout this jurisdiction, every person shall duly resort and attend thereunto respectively upon the Lord's Day and upon such public fast days and days of thanksgiving as are to be generally kept by the appointment of authority." Absences were to result in fines of five shillings each.[1]

I Introspection and the Diary

Despite the importance of church attendance, acts of corporate worship such as the Lord's Supper, admission to the church by public relation, and the requirement that serious sins be publicly confessed, Puritans nonetheless conceived of their religion as a private, personal, intimate experience, in which man and God, and man and his soul were the truly important elements. Preachers always emphasized the need for introspection, for self-examination. Thomas Hooker, for example, taught the virtue of "serious meditation" on one's sins. Meditation is for Hooker "nothing else but a settled exercise of the mind for the further inquiry of a truth, and so the affection of the heart therewith." Meditation means considering the personal relevance of a doctrine; it means the search of the soul for sin and its sources; but it also means the search for signs of grace. It requires time and attention. English Puritans produced many spiritual manuals that urged self-examination. Robert Bolton, for instance, urged, "Let no day pass thee wherein thou dost not call thyself to a strict account. This task, I must confess, is somewhat hard to set on . . . but assuredly the constant use of it shall make a man see better and more comfortable days."[2]

Conversion preaching encouraged self-examination as a means of achieving salvation. But preachers devoted much attention to the importance of self-examination after conversion as well. Although one's fate had been determined by God before all time, one could not be sure even after conversion that one had truly been saved. Thomas Hooker suggested that if people would only see that their hopes of salvation are false, "there were a great deal of likelihood that they would obtain true grace, and so consequently come to be everlastingly saved." Hooker argued that "there is a possibility revealed of God for man to know whether or not he be called of God or not; it is attainable for man to know whether he be in the state of grace or remain still in his natural condition." But he immediately warned his hearers, "Let the unspeakable comfort that issues from this assurance, the endless joy that ariseth hence, make us careful seekers of so great a benefit."[3]

While Puritan preachers put great emphasis on the conversion experience, its time, place, and circumstance, these same preachers were preoccupied with the possibility that one might be mistaken. Assurance was not in fact ever really available. Thomas Shepard declared, "Be always converting, and always converted; turn us again, O Lord. When a man thinks, 'I was humbled and comforted; I will not lay all by and so live on old scraps,' O beware that frame; not that a Christian should be always pulling up foundations, and ever doubting, but to make sure, be always converting, more humble, more sensible of sin, more near Christ Jesus. . . ."[4]

As a means of self-examination, some Puritans kept diaries. These personal documents reveal much about the nature of Puritanism. Self-examination by means of a diary had obvious virtues. The self that examines and the self that is examined could be distinguished as the diarist objectified his experiences, his feelings, his reasonings. What he learned about himself he recorded and by externalizing it felt a greater sense of control. The lonely and isolated task became easier; a regular record gave a gratifying sense of discipline. Here four of the most important diaries will be considered: those of Thomas Shepard (1605-1649), Michael Wigglesworth (1631-1705), Samuel Sewall (1652-1730), and Cotton Mather (1663-1728).[5]

II *Thomas Shepard's Diary*

Thomas Shepard's recently published journal begins with an entry for November 25, 1640, and ends with an entry dated March 30, 1644. (He may have written others, not known to survive.) It is wholly concerned with Shepard's spiritual health. Typically, Shepard begins with uncertainty, either doubts that he is worthy of salvation or doubts that there is a God to save him. His examination of these doubts usually leads to assurance—of a sort. Nearly every weakness is turned to strength. For example, sensing in himself a spirit of "atheism," a "weakness to see or believe God," Shepard reasons that God's having withdrawn faith might have been occasioned by his intending to strengthen Shepard's faith by increasing his sense of need to believe. His meditations also lead him to see the difference between "knowing things by reason and discourse, and by faith, or the spirit of faith." By the former he "saw that a thing was so"; by the latter, he saw "the thing that was so."[6]

Shepard never begins an entry by celebrating his faith. He begins by accounting his spiritual struggles. He sees that he must "die eternally" for his sins, that God was now already "departed and hid his face and did not appear in his love for me." As a consequence he renews his dependence on Christ, so that his "help was in him and faith in him." This sense of dependence is for Shepard deeply comforting. But he is seldom given real assurance. At times he achieves "some measure of faith"; he enjoys "very sweet persuasion" that his work as a minister is "not despised of the Lord." His strongest statement of faith does not record a specific experience: "I have seen God himself and have been ravished to behold him." When and where and how are not explained. But Shepard is continually *seeing*, though much of what he saw was discomforting: "I saw . . . the reason why the Lord left me alone was because I left him alone." His introspective discovery of his deficiency leads him back to God.[7]

Shepard can recognize "full assurance" only conditionally:

I saw an effectual offer was a gift. When God did effectually offer Christ, he gave Christ. In this sacrament I was much troubled about the ground of my faith because I wanted an immediate absolute testimony of special mercy. Yet I looked unto the word and saw (1) if those who look up to Christ for all from him, (2) if those that come to him and seek for supply of all wants from him, (3) if those that receive Christ by election of him above all (as by refusing of the will he is shut out), (4) if receiving of him as my own because called by the gospel to come up to possess him, and so trusting to him—if this or these were faith, that I [had] some cause of being assured that the Lord had forgiven my sins, and the sacrament were a full assurance to me.

Shepard's tortured self-examination leads to no conviction, no real certainty.[8]

The most reliable way, according to Shepard, to know that one is saved is to test one's self by means of the promises of the Bible: "The Lord has spoken peace to some men's hearts thus. 'He that is lost shall be found; he that believes in me shall never hunger; and he that comes to me shall never thirst'; and seeing this, they conclude (the Lord's Spirit helping them, for sometimes they cannot do it) peace. For the major [premise] is the word, the minor [premise] experience, and the conclusion the Lord's Spirit quickening your experience to it." Unlike Anne Hutchinson, who declared that "the ground of her revelation is the immediate revelation of the Spirit and not by the ministry of the word" (as John Winthrop put it), orthodox Puritans believed that revelation should "concur with the word." If assurance is to come from self-examination as to the applicability of the promises in the word, the examiner has to interpret the evidence. Here is the way Shepard reasoned to verify that his experience made him eligible to receive the benefits of the promises:

I considered . . . that if I did make an absolute promise of favor to me a ground of resting upon Christ, that this was a promise made to one out of Christ, and if this was so, then such a promise was a false promise and a delusion, for out of Christ there is no promise of mercy except in the word. And also consequently I must always rest upon a promise to one in a corrupt estate, but if I rested upon conditional promises or such as did follow my coming unto Christ, then the promise was certainly of God, because to one in Christ.

Shepard's conditional IF, a big one, suggests a kind of double jeopardy in which the possibilities of misleading oneself are very great. Shepard's journal indicates that even a dedicated Puritan

minister who practiced self-examination rigorously might not find
lasting comfort in his religion.[9]

III   Michael Wigglesworth's Diary

Michael Wigglesworth, who came to America in 1638 at the age
of seven, was graduated from Harvard in 1651. Minister at Malden,
near Boston, for many years, he is best known as the creator of the
long theological poem The Day of Doom (1662) and other verses.
His diary covers the period from February 1653 to May 1657. While
it deals with a few events in his life, such as a trip to Connecticut,
the entries chiefly concern Wigglesworth's conscience and his
preoccupation with sin—both his own and others'. As the editor of
his diary notes, Wigglesworth as he is to be found in his diary is an
embodiment of the popular caricature of the Puritan, full of zeal,
suspicious of pleasure, wracked by guilt.[10]

He was ever-ready to tell others "of the dangers of pleasure and
how they had like to have been my ruin. Knowing the danger of
them therefore I dissuade both myself and others." He was much
troubled by one who let "his spirit go after pleasures." He was
tormented that his own heart "seeks after sensual contentment,"
that it found pleasure in "this or that creature, this or that project."
Everywhere that he found pleasure (except in God), he found
himself sinning.[11]

Wigglesworth's God is not attractive. God visits him "with bodily
weakness," punishes his spiritual "barrenness with public drought,"
even makes Harvard College suffer because Wigglesworth is not the
good man he ought to be: "Thus I can pull down wrath and destroy
myself and all about me." He finds that God does not answer his
prayers because "I have not been deeply sensible of my own utter
unworthiness." He is "vile"; he has a "hopeless, shiftless soul." He
is "unfit for heaven because he is unfit for earth." Since
Wigglesworth's talent for describing his own sinfulness and corruption is remarkable, one wonders what he might have said about
himself had be been able to write all that he must have wished.[12]

What were Wigglesworth's sins? Not deeds but attitudes: pride,
spiritual deadness, hardness of heart, unspecified fleshly lusts. He is
reminded of the existence of his sins by "the itch and biles breaking
out so as to make me lame," "flatulent vapors that annoy me," "the
spleen." A sickly, small man, Wigglesworth seldom found comfort
in his religion. Occasionally his day goes well, and he finds that he

can thank God. But when he finds God helping him in his activities, he soon recognizes that he is becoming filled with damnable pride in what he has accomplished. While studying philosophy, he records, "I found the Lord so extraordinarily assisting me above and beyond my own folly in quickness of invention and reasoning, that instead of admiring my God I found myself very prone to admire myself, and so like a wretch I turn from grace to wantonness."[13]

Obviously Puritanism is not to be blamed as the sole cause of Wigglesworth's problems. Two sources appear to be, as Steven Kagle has observed, Oedipal and sexual. Wigglesworth in his early twenties tended to draw parallels between his father and his Father. When his father scolded him, or as Wigglesworth put it, when God "makes my father an instrument of so discovering my weak and silly management of every business," his heart "swells against my father and cannot conceive such things to proceed from love." Later he decided that God intended to kick him "out of this world because I have not that natural affection to my natural father but requited him, and all my governors, evil for good." He expected to "be shut out of the world to come because I have rebelled against and dishonored and disregarded my heavenly father, been a viper in his bosom where he nourished me." Here Wigglesworth's pronouns refer seemingly to both parent and God. Naturally, under the circumstances he was greatly afflicted with his sinfulness when he learned that his father was dead: he mourned his "stupid frame of spirit unsensible of God's visitation and my own loss in losing such a friend."[14]

He was equally troubled by his "unnatural filthy lust," "such unresistible torments of carnal lusts until the ejection of seed," his "dreams and self-pollution by night which my soul abhors and mourns for." But both this problem and the former seem less severe when Wigglesworth finds a wife and nine months later finds himself to be a father. After these events his diary has fewer entries and finally breaks off.[15]

Knowing that according to Puritan doctrine he was, like all men, totally depraved, Wigglesworth found it easy to see sin in everything he did. Indeed, by the standard of perfection that he demanded of himself, he was consistently wanting. The things of this world had little to offer, according to Puritan theology; letting them be in any way distracting from God was enough to cause sin. Wigglesworth wholly embraced this concept. Most readers of his diary find its revelation of Wigglesworth's consciousness repulsive;

his poems similarly lack warmth, charity, kindness. Guilt-ridden and sickly, Wigglesworth managed nonetheless to serve with some effectiveness as minister and also as physician to his town until his death at the age of seventy-four. Samuel Sewall's description of him as "learned and pious," "very useful as a physician," suggests that he may have been more attractive to the world in which he traveled than he was to himself.[16]

IV Samuel Sewall's Diary

Sewall himself is the author of the most famous Puritan diary. Much more massive than either Shepard's or Wigglesworth's, Sewall's diary covers the period 1674-1729, years when the influence of Puritan ideas declined. Sewall was not a clergyman, though as a Harvard graduate he had received a minister's education and had many clerical friends. A businessman, he married the daughter of John Hull, a leading merchant; later the wealth he inherited permitted him to shift his field of activity to civic service. Having served as a judge at the famous Salem Village witch trials of 1692, Sewall eventually saw that he himself had been guilty of evil in his condemnation of the "witches" and publicly acknowledged his error. Besides his career in law, which led to services as chief justice of Massachusetts Bay, he wrote several pamphlets, notably one advocating the freeing of Negro slaves, *The Selling of Joseph*.[17]

Sewall's diary reveals a pious man but not one devoted to the kind of soul-searching that Shepard and Wigglesworth had undertaken. Mostly this Puritan-Yankee records his daily activities, and as an historical record his diary is invaluable. While he did not conceive of his diary as an account of his backsliding, his doubts, and his experiences of grace, Sewall did register in a striking fashion his perception of God's hand in the events of everyday life. For example, when he spent the night in the Charlestown house originally owned by John Harvard, he "was affected to consider how long ago God had made him provision for my comfortable lodging that night."[18]

Sewall seldom struggled over religious issues except for the question of how to read Biblical prophecies, a subject he discussed in two publications. He did not expect to have disturbing religious experiences. "Look not," he told himself, "to the earnestness of your motions but the regularity of them." For the sake of regularity he tried to see every experience in a religious perspective. In England, when he saw "several graves open and the bones thick on top," he prayed that his "flesh, bones, and spirits" might be improved, since they are "so soon to become useless." When he discovered to his discomfort that the bottom of his chamber pot had come out while he was using it in bed, he recorded in his diary, "How unexpectedly a man may be exposed! There's no security but in God, who is to be sought in prayer." He could be stirred on occasion, such as the sudden strickening of his wife, who died to Sewall's great astonishment. He concluded that he had "cause to be ashamed of my sin and to loath myself for it, and retired into my pew."[19]

Death seems to surround Sewall. He visits the dying; he records unusual deaths; he attends dozens of funerals; he keeps death ever before him. His attitude was doubtless shaped by the Puritan concept that death was a crucial religious experience. The search for religious assurance, assurance of salvation, reached a climax as death drew near. Even the dedicated Increase Mather, whom Sewall visited on his death bed to offer words of comfort, was deeply "concerned with so much fear and trembling lest he should be deceived at last," his son Cotton reports. (Increase had devoted much attention, his son notes, to the question of assurance, for "no care could be too much to prevent our being deceived in that important matter.") Puritans feared death for many reasons: their sense of their own depravity, their belief that God was absolutely just, and their fear of hell.[20]

Sewall does not himself record often his reflections on death, for the diary is sparing of introspection. He records a routinized piety, the fruit of a Puritanism well established, become even a convention. To cope with the anxieties of life, Puritan ministers prescribed responses, patterns that reduced the tensions that earlier Puritans had contended with, especially those associated with death and burial. In the late seventeenth century an elaborate ceremonial for a funeral was developed in New England. The English Puritans had reduced funerals to simple affairs, and the *Directory for the Publique Worship of God* of 1645, prepared as an outcome of the Westminster Assembly, ordered that "when any person departeth this life, let the dead body, upon the day of burial, be decently attended from the house to the place appointed for public burial, and there interred, without any ceremony." In New England the body was frequently displayed in church. Gloves were sent as an invitation to the funeral. One man collected over three thousand pair, and Sewall accumulated over three score funeral rings carved with death heads, coffins, and skeletons. Usually, perhaps as a consequence of the effectiveness of the routines, Sewall seems to have been relatively unaffected by death. Compared with earlier Puritans, Samuel Sewall was remarkably lacking in self-consciousness, though he is in many ways an attractive person, curious, alert, well-meaning.[21]

V Cotton Mather's Diary

Samuel Sewall's contemporary Cotton Mather was a profoundly religious man, dedicated to the ideals of the Puritan founders of New England. (His role in the history of Puritanism is so important that he is the subject of an extended discussion elsewhere in this study.) His diary, a very full one, differs from the others treated here in that it was intended to be read as a record of his religious experiences. This fact may explain something of the qualities of style, its feverishness, its efforts to suggest rapture. But the author was also a strikingly imaginative, eccentrically emotional personality. Unlike Shepard, Wigglesworth, and Sewall, Mather records frequent direct revelations of God, often brought on by long vigils, fasting, and self-mortification. He saw himself as God's agent, even at times as a version of Jesus Christ. While Mather's mysticism and profound emotional excitement differentiate him from most Puritans, the importance given religious experience in New England not infrequently resulted in enthusiastic responses. (It also sometimes led to despair and suicide as well.) Mather's emotionalism is somewhat balanced by a side of Puritanism that developed fairly late. The very demanding moral standards of Puritanism specified precisely what sins of commission were to be avoided; the moral code was much less specific about sins of omission. Mather emphasized doing good. Though his ultimate objective was the universal triumph of the Protestant Reformation all over the world, even in Asia, he was devoted to small, specific acts of charity, to collecting money for the relief of victims of the great Boston fire of 1711, to reducing the smallpox plague through innoculation, to efforts, often effective, to settle quarrels. One of Mather's most influential books is *Bonifacius: An Essay Upon the Good,* in which he urged the creation of voluntary associations to reform morals, and in which he specifies how schoolmasters, lawyers, magistrates, and others can become more useful to humanity. All such acts of charity are to be undertaken not as substitutes for piety but as means by which a Christian can use the grace God has given him.[22]

Pages and pages, hundreds of them, in Mather's diary list "G.D.'s," each a "Good Devised," each an answer to the question he determined in 1711 to put to himself each day: "What shall I render to the Lord?" Each is a good intended, and one can only assume, since the diary does not indicate, that most of the plans were carried out. Mather plans to provide clothes for an aged man, to lecture to a group of young gamblers, to visit his sister-in-law, who is about to give birth to a baby. Some "goods" are personal, as when he decides that he must think sacrificially about everything that he finds dear and valuable to himself. Through sacrifice he expected to become "a weaned Christian . . . prepared for all events."[23]

Mather took enormous satisfaction in keeping a diary. He records, ostensibly to himself, "I can't call to mind any one person who has injured me but I have requited them good." He can record that his dying wife could find no fault in him, that a visitor reported to him, "All the men that have any virtue or reason in them, I find, love you and value you, and honor you, but all the base people, who are scandalous for vice and wickedness, hate you and can't give you a good word."[24]

Mather conceived of his life to be devoted to service. He prays that he might be favored "in special endeavors to serve the name of my Lord Jesus Christ, wherein I am now engaged." He conceives of the writing and publishing of books as a form of service. Prostrate in the dust of his study (a posture that according to his diary he frequently assumed), Mather receives "the Spirit and the Angel of the Lord," who assures him that soon he is to do "a special service of great consequence for the name of my Lord Jesus Christ, which, as yet, I know not what it is."[25]

Mather conceived of his program of "goods devised" to be a consequence of God's grace dwelling within him. He records a conversation with a young minister who thought himself unconverted. Mather began by asking:

"I pray, sir, what is it that stands upon the shelf before you?"
"A repeating clock, and a very curious one."
"What use do you think I will put it to?"
"Sir, you'll assign it a convenient and honorable place in your house and put it to the noble use of measuring your time."
"How do you know that I shall not make it a stool to sit upon, a block to tread upon, a backlog to be thrown into my fire?"

"Sir, the workmanship of it makes it appear to be intended for no such miserable use."

"Well then, have not you upon your soul a divine workmanship far more excellent than the most curious clock-work in the world? A work of grace is a work of God, even of him who does nothing in vain. You find in yourself a disposition, a strong disposition and inclination to glorify God, and serve the interests of the Lord Jesus Christ, and slay all sin as being most contrary unto him. This is work of grace. You know no delight comparable to that of serving the Lord Jesus Christ. God has wrought this in you, and herein he has wrought you, for that self-same thing, of being to the praise of His glory forever. What use can you think He will now put you to but that [of] serving the Lord Jesus Christ in His heavenly world? Such a piece of workmanship (created unto good works) as what is wrought in you was never intended to be thrown into the fire of Hell. No, there is no use of it there. God intends you an heavenly use, undoutedly."

Doing good was for Mather profoundly gratifying: "I take an unspeakable pleasure in all manner of beneficence. If I can see opportunities to do good unto any, I need no arguments to move me to it; I do it naturally, delightfully, with rapture." The observation is persuasive, much more so than one in which he protests, "I have no fondness at all for applause and honor in the world. It is with a sort of horror if I perceive myself applauded. I have a dread of being honored."[26]

One source of Mather's assurance that he was of the elect is his frequent sense of what he called "a particular faith": a sense that God hears his petition and responds, "I will do something towards that temporal blessing which may show thee how able I, how willing I am to gratify thee." The diary is full of particular faiths: he is given a conviction, for example, that his daughter, near death, will recover. His faith is sorely tried when he has to wait years for the fulfillment of his faith that his huge *Magnalia Christi Americana* will finally be published. While often depressed by his sinfulness, Mather records little of the anxiety about whether he has been saved that so fills Shepard's journal. In fact, many of Mather's particular faiths provided him with an anxiety of a sort that he seems actually to have needed. Was his faith well grounded or a delusion? As Perry Miller explains, the search for a particular faith could permit Mather to "recapture those ardors of soul the founders had experienced. . . ." A particular faith also reasserted God's power.[27]

Since he suffered many defeats especially through his last years, the sense of assurance of God's favor given him by his many particular faiths must have provided much-needed sustenance. In 1724, when he was sixty-one, Mather catalogued "the recompenses" of his "poor essays at well doing." His list of fourteen items includes the following:

What has a gracious Lord given me to do that I may be a blessing to my relatives? I keep a catalogue of them, and not a week passes me without some good devised for some or other of them, till I have taken all of them under my cognizance.

AND YET, where is the man who hath been tormented with such monstrous relatives? Job said, "I am brother to dragons."

What has a gracious Lord given me to do in the writing of many books for the advancing of piety and the promoting of his kingdom, glory to God in the highest and good will among men? There are, I suppose, more than three hundred and thirty of them.

AND YET, I have had more books written against me, more pamphlets to traduce me and reproach me and belie me than any man that I know in the world.

What has a gracious Lord given me to do in alms and in disbursements on pious uses? For whole years together, not one day has passed me in which I have not been able to say that I have done something that way.

AND YET, though I am strangely provided for, yet I am a very poor man. I have not a foot of land upon earth. Except a library and a little household stuff, I have nothing upon earth. And this also I am now offering to my creditors to satisfy my debts whereof I never did myself owe a farthing. My very library, the darling of my little enjoyments, is demanded from me. 'Tis inexpressible, how much this condition pleases me, gladdens me!

The reversals he cites had truly occurred. This strange, introspective man did not know himself, despite his diary-keeping—did not know that his deep-died Puritanism made him appear ridiculous to many of his contemporaries, especially in the eighteenth century. Mather's faith permitted him to see that if he were "a man of sorrows and acquainted with grief," that very fact permitted him to write that "A glorious Christ has revealed himself to me, has conferred himself on me, has taken possession of me." By casting himself in the role of a suffering savior, he was able to survive.[28]

The diaries of Shepard, Wigglesworth, and Mather show men under great emotional pressure. Religion was not merely a matter of the spirit; it dominated the body as well, the whole being. If it offered comfort, it created profound anxiety as well. None of these

three diarists makes an attractive impression. As they poured their
energies into introspection, these active, creative people become
egotists before our eyes: their only concern is themselves. Sacvan
Bercovitch's observations are to the point: the "urge for self-denial
stems from the very subjectivism of their outlook, . . . [so that]
their humility is coextensive with personal assertion." We see "the
individual affirming his identity by turning against his power of
self-affirmation." Samuel Sewall is exceptional: his diary was a
record, not a place where he undertook self-evaluation. His moral
outlook, his routinized piety, and his preoccupation with death
nevertheless reflect his Puritanism in significant ways.[29]

Puritanism never taught withdrawal from the world. There were
no Puritan monasteries; people were expected to live in families,
with relatives if not with parents and children. Solitary living was
forbidden. During the years 1669 - 1677 Massachusetts persecuted
sixty people for living alone; similar laws were on the books in New
Haven, Rhode Island, and Connecticut. Though one might struggle
by oneself, he was expected to live in community, close to others.
Puritans lived in small towns where there was much interaction
between individuals. Perhaps the Puritan habit of introspection was
less unhealthy than it seems because people lived much closer
together three centuries ago.[30]

CHAPTER 7

The Decline of Puritanism

THE power and influence of Puritanism began to decline significantly during the last third of the seventeenth century, though Puritanism was a long time a-dying, if it is dead yet. There were many causes for the decline. Puritan ministers lost their status as the exclusive religious leaders of Massachusetts and Connecticut. Other religious groups, chiefly Baptist and Anglican, began to compete for members with Congregational churches. In time the political franchise was not restricted to members of Congregational churches: political power became available to other than orthodox church members. Secular attitudes grew more dominant as commercial leaders achieved power. They brought New England into closer contact with the world outside the Puritan commonwealth, and, outside, the winds of doctrine blew from many directions. New philosophical and scientific attitudes began to influence and to soften such tough-minded Puritan doctrines as total depravity. Calvinism was gradually to give way to Arminianism and eventually to Unitarianism, though well into the nineteenth century many Congregational churches were Calvinist at least in principle. Puritanism became almost wholly a conservative force. The unity that it advocated was impossible in a world becoming the contemporary pluralistic one. This complicated story cannot be adequately told here; yet a few episodes and personalities may be sketched to indicate what went on.

I The Erosion of Puritan Exclusiveness

New England Puritanism defined early and narrowly its acceptable limits of toleration by its exile of Roger Williams and Anne Hutchinson. In his debate with Williams in the 1640s, John Cotton described in a positive way how he and other Puritans were attempting to build a uniquely harmonious society founded on a voluntary covenant. Another Puritan spokesman described the Massachusetts Bay policy rather more bluntly: " . . . all Familists, Antinomians, Anabaptists, and other Enthusiasts shall have free liberty to keep away from us, and such as will come to be gone as fast as they can, the sooner the better." For Massachusetts Puritans truth was ONE: toleration meant permitting error. In 1658 the General Court made even more explicit what should have been already well known when it declared that "no person shall publicly or constantly preach to any company of people, whether in church society or not . . . where any two organic churches, council of state, or General Court shall declare their dissatisfaction thereat. . . ."[1]

The policy of exclusion was not merely set forth on paper. In 1651 three Rhode Island Baptists visited Lynn in the Massachusetts Bay colony, at the request of a former member of the Newport church, to hold a worship service. All three men were arrested. One was given thirty lashes, another fined. In the following year, one of the three published a report on his experience, *Ill Newes from New England*. Quakers were given similar treatment even before the General Court passed a law providing that any shipmaster who brought a Quaker into the colony would be fined one hundred pounds, any colonist possessing a Quaker book would be fined five pounds, and any Quaker reaching Massachusetts would be arrested, whipped, and transported. A stricter law soon replaced this severe one, and soon four Quakers who went as missionaries to the Bay colony notwithstanding its attitude were punished by hanging. The treatment received by the Quakers was advertised by George Bishop in *New-England Judged* (London, 1661), and in that same year, with monarchy now reestablished in England, Charles II issued an order forbidding the Massachusetts practice.[2]

Protestantism was splintering in the seventeenth century, and religious diversity was leading to religious toleration in some parts of the world. In New England religious radicals of several kinds found haven in Rhode Island, which received a patent as "Providence Plantation" in 1644. Its instrument of government, adopted in 1647, explained that "otherwise than thus, what is herein forbidden, all men may walk as their consciences persuade them, every one in the name of his God." Baptist churches were created there, and the newly created Society of Friends became well established, with its leader George Fox visiting the Friends or Quakers in 1672. Anglicans, too, were there by 1700.[3]

The churches of Connecticut were almost wholly dominated by Congregationalists in the seventeenth century, with only one group of dissenters to be found, at New London. The presence of a tolerating colony close by made Massachusetts and Connecticut Puritans uncomfortable. Massachusetts leaders found their policies were treated unsympathetically by the English government and a sovereign who might be able, as his predecessor was not, to give attention to the question of how his subjects were faring in the Puritan commonwealth over the seas. In Massachusetts Anglicans were not tolerated, though, as late as Cotton Mather, Congregational spokesmen who had never been Separatists described themselves as members of the Church of England. Many colonists were now complaining to the royal government that the Massachusetts Bay leaders were persecuting non-Congregationalists, especially in what is now New Hampshire and Maine, portions of which Massachusetts then governed. Puritan leaders were determined to preserve their sovereignty despite the complaints, including the published ones, and as a first step Governor John Endecott wrote to Charles II, reminding him that "Our liberty to walk in the faith of the Gospel was the cause of our transporting ourselves . . . over the Atlantic Ocean into this vast and waste wilderness." Only a noncommittal reply was received.[4]

To get assurance from the king that they would be permitted to keep their now well established sovereignty, the General Court of Massachusetts Bay sent Simon Bradstreet and the Reverend John Norton to London in 1662. To their satisfaction, Charles II consented to confirm the colony's charter, but he required the Massachusetts Bay government to permit those who wished to do so to use the Book of Common Prayer without prejudice and ordered that "all persons of good and honest lives and conversation be admitted to the sacrament of the Lord's Supper according to the said Book of Common Prayer, and their children to baptism." He also ordered that "all freeholders of competent estates, not vicious in religion, (though of different persuasions concerning church government) might have their vote in the election of all officers, civil or military." In response the Court did little except to broaden the franchise slightly, and then to explain that it had acted in keeping with the king's order "as far as doth consist with conscience of our duty towards God and the just liberties and privileges of our patent."[5]

Despite this rigid stand, the situation in Massachusetts gradually changed. Two of the founders of a Baptist church in Charlestown in 1665 were imprisoned for a year, and in 1668 the General Court ordered them banished, but when sixty-six persons signed a protest, the Court relented. By 1679 the Baptists were able to build a meeting house in Boston. In 1682 the General Court declared that there were no restrictions against the establishment of Baptist churches.[6]

II   *The Old Charter Lost*

Some internal divisions on questions of religious policy were in part responsible for the changes that occurred, but pressure from England was the important factor. While Massachusetts Bay officials were able to prevent outside interference for a time, Charles II eventually sent commissioners to New England, who reported what was happening there. For Massachusetts, the commissioners had no kind words:

They of this colony say that Charles I granted them a charter as a warrant against himself and successors, and so long as they pay the fifth of all gold and silver ore they are not obliged to the King but by civility. They hope to tire the King, the Lord Chancellor, and the Secretaries, and say they can easily spin out seven years by writing, and before that time change may come; nay, some have dared to say, Who knows what the event of this Dutch war may be? They furnished Cromwell with many instruments out of their corporation and college, and solicited him . . . to be declared a free state, and now style and believe themselves to be so. . . . Those whom they will not admit to communion, they compel to come to their sermons, by forcing from them five shillings for every neglect, yet these men thought their own paying of one shilling for not coming to prayers in England an insupportable tyranny. They have put to death and banished many Quakers on pain of death, and then executed them for returning, and have beaten some to a jelly, and been exceeding cruel to others, and say the King allows it in his letters to them, yet they pray constantly for their persecuted brethren in England. Many things in their laws derogatory to his Majesty's honor, the commissioners desired might be altered, but nothing as yet [is] done. . . . At Cambridge they have a wooden college . . . . It may be feared that this college may afford as many schismatics to the church and the corporation as many rebels to the King as formerly they have done, if not timely prevented.[7]

To present its case, Massachusetts sent agents to London but, jealous of its cherished prerogatives—legal or illegal—gave no authority to the representatives. In frustration, the King threatened to revoke the colony's charter unless it submitted to his demands. While many people in Massachusetts, especially merchants, favored submission, Massachusetts leaders after much delaying decided to employ a London attorney to defend the charter. The effort proved unsuccessful, and in 1684 Massachusetts lost its charter. The King sent Sir Edmund Andros to serve as royal governor of the Dominion of New England, which included Massachusetts. During his regime, some significant changes took place, such as the establishment of King's Chapel, an Anglican church, in Boston. But the Glorious Revolution dethroned the Stuarts and made Andros's tenure brief.[8]

The man who has been called "the foremost American Puritan," Increase Mather, was now sent to negotiate with the new royal government for a new charter. He sought to preserve the independence of Massachusetts, which had made Puritan power possible. But his success was far from complete. Under the new charter Massachusetts was definitely a colony, and with its sovereignty, Massachusetts was to lose—not overnight, but gradually—its uniqueness. Why did the commonwealth not declare its independence? Presumably because to do so would have meant that it would have been seized by France, then powerfully established in the St. Lawrence and Mississippi River valleys and at war with England beginning in 1689. Massachusetts found itself very vulnerable: its attempt to take Montreal under the leadership of Sir William Phips had failed, and French-incited Indians were attacking settlers in Maine, which was under Massachusetts government. The colony had been drained financially by its military efforts. It was forced to submit to the terms of the new charter, though many Puritan ministers, recognizing that the new charter reduced their powers substantially, called the returning Increase Mather a renegade.[9]

That Massachusetts did not wholly lose its power of self-government under the new charter was the result of the need of William III to enjoy popular support in Massachusetts in his war against the French. But Massachusetts now had a royal governor, authorized to veto any legislation passed by the General Court, which was elected by the citizenry. The governor himself was under the control of the crown, which issued instructions on both matters of policy and specific issues. The charter had a loophole that left the General Court power, since the charter made no provision for a fund for payment of royal officials. With the power of the purse, the Court could even force the governor to resign.[10]

For the Puritans, important aspects of the new charter included the liberty of conscience that it gave to all except Catholics and the extension of the franchise, which had been limited to Congregational church members. Increase Mather admitted to his diary that the new charter meant the loss of "all the old dearest privileges." His assessment proved to be valid, for soon Massachusetts was governed by Joseph Dudley, son of a founder, Governor Thomas Dudley, and brother of Anne Bradstreet, but now a royalist. (He had served briefly as governor before Andros arrived, and had been imprisoned when Andros's government fell.) Gradually—and for tradition-minded Puritans painfully—Massachusetts came under royal control.[11]

III   The Growth of Secularism and Cosmopolitanism

Economically, the Puritan commonwealth was able to be self-sufficient during the first dozen years as a result of the wealth brought in by newcomers who purchased from those who were already settled cattle and commodities they needed to establish themselves. When the Puritans in England began to gain power in the 1640s, the exodus of immigrants to New England quickly stopped, and New England suffered depression. Some men had made money from the fur trade, which had led to the creation of western settlements, such as Springfield. But furs brought money to only a few people, and the supply of animal pelts was soon exhausted. New England now had to depend on hard-headed businessmen, despite the fact that such men were considered subversive by many Puritan leaders. Edward Johnson commented that God "hath purposely picked out this people for a pattern of purity and soundness of doctrine as well as discipline, that all such may find a refuge among you, and let not any merchants, innkeepers, taverners, and men of trade in hope of gain fling open the gates so wide as that by letting in all sorts you mar the work of Christ intended."[12]

The forerunners of the Massachusetts Bay colonists had been fishermen, sent out by the Dorchester Company of Adventurers in 1623. But fishing was not an important source of income for some years after the colony was established in the 1630s. It became important as trade became necessary for economic survival. One of the first successful ventures in trade by Bay businessmen was the shipment of fish to the Azores, Canaries, Madeira, and Spain. Eventually merchants created a complicated system of trade involving the shipment of pipe staves, tall trees for ship masts, and fish from New England, sugar and tobacco from the Caribbean, black slaves from Africa, and wine from Spain and the wine islands. The effect of this trade was to bring wealth to some New Englanders, but it also brought New Englanders into contact with the outside world. Puritans who had sought to isolate their commonwealth in order to create and preserve purity now saw economic power going to a class of men who were often not sympathetic with the ideals of the covenanted community. Merchants eventually could dictate prices and terms of credit, though for a time the General Court sought to control the economy, according to such principles as those set forth by John Cotton, who in 1639 had declared, "A man may not sell above the current price. . . ." Merchants expanded their influence by buying up large parcels of land. They knew that the Massachusetts of intolerance was bad for their business image, and so they sought—as early as 1645—to eliminate the laws that prevented those unsympathetic with Puritanism from settling in Massachusetts.[13]

By the 1670s ministers were frequently attacking the merchants because of the secular spirit they were creating in New England. In his election day sermon for 1663, *The Cause of God and His People in New England,* the Reverend John Higginson of Salem declared: "My fathers and brethren, this is never to be forgotten, that New-England is originally a plantation of religion, not a plantation of trade. Let merchants and such as are increasing *cent per cent* remember this. Let others that have come over since at several times understand this, that worldly gain was not the end and design of the people of New England, but religion."[14]

But the capitalistic spirit of the merchants also found encouragement in Puritan teaching. As Max Weber, R. H. Tawney, and David Little have persuasively shown, the Puritan emphasis on vocation encouraged individualism and competitiveness at a time when the application of energies in business was likely to have positive results. Men were expected to have a vocation or calling to which they would devote themselves without stint. William Ames, the highly influential Puritan teacher, argued that men had an obligation to exert themselves to avoid poverty. William Adams, preaching in the 1670s and 1680s, argued that the believer "hath much business to do in and about the world, which he is vigorously to attend, and he hath in that in the world upon which he is to bestow affection." Another preacher of the same period argued that "Man is made for labor, and not for idleness." Joshua Moody was more specific. "It is rational," he urged, "that men should lay out money where they may have the most suitable commodities and best pennyworths." The religious ideals of the founders were giving way to both the action of hostile forces from without and the consequences of fundamental Puritan teachings from within. Perry Miller described the situation as a paradox: "The more the people worked in the right spirit, the more they transformed the society into something they never intended; the more diligently they labored on the frontier, in the field, in the countinghouse, or on the banks of Newfoundland, the more surely they produced what according to the standards of the founders was a decay of religion and a corruption of morals." Miller ignores the coming of non-Puritan merchants to New England, but he argues persuasively that Puritanism had within itself the seeds of its own destruction in its teachings of individual enterprise. [15]

Boston was the first town to witness a significant rise of the merchant class. They sided with the Hutchinsonians at the time of the Antinomian controversy, and some left Boston as a result. Those who remained were looked upon with suspicion by the inhabitants of other towns, who were soon resentful of Boston's prosperity. Since the merchants were a small minority in the General Court, they were kept from power there. The opposition between Boston merchants and traditional Puritans in other towns created in Boston—and later in other commercial centers, such as Charlestown and Salem—two contrasting sets of values. As Bernard Bailyn has observed, the old Puritan values of stability, order, and discipline were now confronting the merchants' values of mobility, growth, and enjoyment of life. When at the end of the century England finally broke the absolute Puritan dominance in the Massachusetts Bay colony, the merchants saw that they had at last an opportunity to gain power in the government of the colony. [6]

The merchants' sense of group identity came not only from mutual interests but also by marriage. In Boston they had a social organization, The Ancient and Honorable Artillery Company. At the very end of the century a group of Boston merchants created their own church, the story of which provides a revealing chapter in the history of New England Puritanism. In January 1698 some merchants decided that it was time to establish a church that would be consonant with their values, which were more liberal than those of churches identified with the traditions of the New England Way. At this time conservative Puritans were in control of all the Boston churches. James Allen was pastor of the First Church of Boston, Increase and Cotton Mather were at the North (Second) Church, and Samuel Willard was at the Third Church (Old South). The founders of the new Brattle Street Church called as their pastor Benjamin Colman, then living in England and preaching at a variety of Presbyterian churches, especially at Bath, where he came to know people of fashion. A graduate of Harvard College in the class of 1692, Colman had studied with William Brattle and John Leverett, who had dominated Harvard during Increase Mather's term abroad as negotiator for the new charter; both teachers had inculcated into their students what they called "an enlarged catholic spirit." (They encouraged the reading of such works as those of the Anglican rationalist Archbishop Tillotson.) The invitation to Colman specifically requested that he be ordained in England, whereas the New England Way prescribed that a man was made a minister by the church that called him. Colman was duly ordained by members of the London Presbytery, but he seems not to have understood the full significance of what he was doing, how much he was going against the tradition. Moreover, he failed to obtain ordination at the hands of the prominent ministers that the Brattle Street founders had expected to be available.[17]

The new church was to depart from tradition in several other ways. It did not require a public relation for church membership. (Benjamin Colman's brother wanted membership to depend on character.) It included in the worship service reading from the Bible without comment. Moreover, when the ministers of the area made the traditional request that the founders submit their plans for approval, they ignored the request. Instead Colman and the founders published a Manifesto that was widely disseminated.[18]

The creation of the church and the Manifesto brewed a tempest in a teapot. Cotton Mather in his diary wrote with chagrin that certain articles in the Manifesto "utterly subvert our churches and unite an ill party through all the country to throw all into confusion on the first opportunity." One Boston wit, less disturbed than Mather, wrote these verses:

> Relations are Rattle with Brattle and Brattle,
>   Lord Bro'r mayn't command,
> But Mather and Mather had rather and rather

> The good old way should stand.
> Saints Cotton and Hooker, Oh look down and look here
> Where's Platform, Way, and Keys?
>
> . . . .
>
> Our merchants cum Mico do stand sacro vico,
> Our churches turn genteel,
> Our parsons grow trim and trig with wealth, wine and wig
> And their heads are covered with meal.

Indeed, the Cambridge Platform, John Cotton's *Way of the Churches* and his *Keyes to the Kingdom of Heaven*, the traditional Congregational statements of policy, were giving way through the influence of such genteel merchants as John Mico and the Brattle brothers. The Lord Brethren of the clergy, such as Increase and Cotton Mather, could do nothing about it. Finally, to retain at least a show of unity among Boston churches, the Mathers, father and son, attended a day of prayer at the new church.[19]

Colman brought to Boston something of the spirit of the age as he had absorbed it in London. An elegant preacher who admired the poets Alexander Pope and Edmund Waller, Colman taught a version of the old Calvinist theology, but Calvinism rationalized and softened. He wrote of himself, "I have always openly owned myself something of a Presbyterian under our Congregational form, and my people have freely allowed me my latitude." Colman preached morality, rational morality. "No man," he declared from his pulpit, "is made for himself and his own private affairs but to serve, profit, and benefit others. We are manifestly formed for society and designed by our great creator for mutual dependence in the serviceableness unto each other here in the body. Both the safety and the pleasure of life depend upon our joint proposing and pursuing this design." Invoking pleasure as a basis for morality was, to say the least, untraditional in Boston.[20]

Benjamin Colman's ordination and career at the Brattle Street Church were milestones in the decline of Puritanism. Perhaps even more subversive of the traditional New England Way were the teachings and writings of Solomon Stoddard, of Northampton (1643 - 1729). Stoddard conceived of the Lord's Supper as a means of conversion, and he denied that the Bible was a valid basis for the concept of a church covenant. The Mathers found his ideas more subversive than those of Colman, who eventually became a respected member of the Boston clerical community.[21]

IV *Friction and Disharmony in Connecticut*

The cultural center of Puritanism was Massachusetts Bay. But very early it spread elsewhere. In Connecticut, Puritanism was established as early as the 1630s. Thomas Hooker's presence was very important in Hartford, but his influence did not extend to the other towns established along the Connecticut River. There it was friction, not harmony, that was characteristic: contentions between ministers—and between ministers and congregations, usurpations of power by congregations, and lack of agreement even on theories of church order. This disunity was deepened when Connecticut churches debated the adoption of the half-way covenant, seen by many of the laity at first as a ministerial innovation, later as an attractive means for diluting the authority of the churches. The adoption in the early eighteenth century of the Saybrook Platform, by which the clergy attempted to regain their power, never accomplished what its creators had expected it would. The establishment of Yale eventually made the Connecticut Valley safe for Calvinism, though even Yale was not safe from assaults, for in 1722 its rector, two tutors, and four ministers from nearby declared their allegiance to the Church of England.[22]

V *Cotton Mather Looks Both Ways*

The story of the last days of Puritanism's power in Massachusetts is inextricably interwoven with the career of Cotton Mather, son of Increase, grandson of the illustrious founders John Cotton and Richard Mather. Mather was a loyal son and grandson, full of—even to the point of feeling burdened with—filial piety. He was also a man of his time. His career is a complex one, but three of his many books may be considered here: *Magnalia Christi Americana* (1702), *The Christian Philosopher* (1721), and *Manuductio ad Ministerium* (1726). All three illustrate well the extent to which he looked both backwards and forwards.[23]

Magnalia Christi Americana; or The Ecclesiastical History of New England. In Seven Books is a massive tome. Editions after the first one have occupied two volumes; a new one will occupy several more. The seven books treat the settlement of New England, lives of the governors and the leading ministers, the story of Harvard College and some of its graduates, the history of the churches, "remarkable providences," and disturbances in the churches. Written in a baroque style very different from the earlier Puritan plain style, the *Magnalia* shows heavy borrowings from Mather's "Quotidiana," his mammoth collection of notes from his reading. Written as an epic, the *Magnalia* draws attention to the demanding task that Mather had given himself, parallel to that of Homer, DuBartas, Milton, and Virgil, especially the latter two. The work is full of puns, anagrams, and citations from recondite and obscure sources.[24]

Mather seems to have understood that the tradition he celebrated way dying. He wrote, "Whether New-England may live anywhere else or not, it must live in our history." Despite its pedantry, its complex style, and its phrases from ancient languages, the work lives because of its energy. It is also a remarkable exercise in myth-making. The jeremiads of the second generation had told of the Golden Age of New England's founders. Mather makes them larger-than-life epic heroes. He tells of the New Englanders' departure from England as an exile from depravity and corruption, an exile from Babylon, Egypt, Rome, Ur. His account of their crossing the Atlantic likewise becomes amplified, mythologized. The founding fathers are elevated: Winthrop is Nehemias Americanus, John Winthrop Jr. is Hermes Christianus, and William Bradford is Galeacius Secundus. Mather is at once writing lamentation and prophecy; his work is the ultimate jeremiad, reminding New Englanders again and again of their backsliding from the glorious tradition from which they have departed. At the same time Mather foresees the imminence of the millenium, when Christ will begin his rule. Because Mather's imagination so dominates the work, a recent critic has written that the continuing value of the *Magnalia* "lies in its contribution to the myth-making tradition of American literature."[25]

No one was more aware than Cotton Mather that New England was a unique place, the New Israel. But even in the *Magnalia*, Mather had written " 'Tis possible that our Lord Jesus Christ carried some thousands of reformers into the retirements of an American desert . . . on purpose that . . . he might there . . . give a specimen of many good things which he would have his churches elsewhere aspire and arise unto. And this being done, he knows not whether there be not all done that New-England was planted for, and whether the Plantation may not, soon after this, come to nothing." New Englanders could not, especially after the loss of the charter, perceive themselves as the vanguard of a great movement in Christian history, and they would not conceive of themselves as provincials, though they truly were. Benjamin Colman's elegant style of preaching went against the old Puritan plain style, but elegance soon won the day, for the obvious reason that it was fashionable in England, from which New England was not now so separate. More important in the decline of Puritanism is the fact that clergymen, including Mather, were turning away from the dogmatic theology that had so dominated Puritan thought for some seventy years. The divisions that had been created within the churches of New England could be healed, many began to feel, if men would focus their attention on a few fundamental articles of religion as a basis for practical piety. Such a change of emphasis did not require, as Mather and his fellow inheritors of the Puritan tradition saw it, an *abandonment* of orthodox Calvinism, covenant theology, and the New England Way. It merely required *neglect* of the old principles in favor of ecumenicity and the religion of the heart.[26]

The new piety that Mather and his fellow ministers began to teach owed something to the reports from London of the formation there of societies for improving manners and morals. It also owed something to Cotton Mather's penchant for correspondence even with divines in Lutheran Germany, where there was developing a pietism that has been called "the most powerful force of modern German intellectual history." Thus in 1716 we find Cotton Mather writing to a German chaplain at the English court, "I rejoice to find the *Magnalia Christi Americana* fallen into your hands, and I verily believe that American Puritanism to be so much of a piece with Frederician Pietism [the teachings of the Frederican University of Halle] that if it were possible for the book to be transferred unto our friends in the Lower Saxony, it would find some acceptance and be a little to their glorious intention." Though he was a provincial who never left New England, Mather had a worldwide correspondence and saw his work in Boston as part of an international effort. He especially identified himself with the educational reforms of the new University of Halle.[27]

While Mather's interest in educational reform can be documented from a variety of sources, it is most conveniently set forth in a work profoundly influenced by the new pietism and the example of Halle, *Manuductio ad Ministerium. Directions for a Candidate of the Ministry* (Boston, 1726). Mather sought to create change through his book. In it he rejected much of the Puritan educational tradition, such as logic, which he judged to be a waste of time; metaphysics, with its "cobwebs"; and ethics, which as taught at Harvard he thought to be "a vile thing." He considered historical writings far more important, and he was an enthusiast of Newtonian science. In brief, what Mather would have ministers study is what can be known, or, as K. M. Woody has put it, "the careful delimitation of the realm of reason and debate to what can be known practically and experimentally, and described in terms agreeable to all." This dramatic shift on the part of the man who thought of himself as the spokesman for the tradition of the Puritan founders suggests that important changes were taking place in New England.[28]

Another indication of change in New England and of the decline of Puritanism is the publication of Mather's *The Christian Philosopher* (London, 1721). Mather had long been interested in science. In his early twenties he had begun reading the *Transactions* of the Royal Society of London and the *Ephemirides* of its German counterpart. He collected what he called "Curiosa Americana," on which he prepared fifty-nine lengthy reports to the Royal Society, which eventually elected him to membership. (He was the first Fellow to have been born in the colonies.) In the early 1720s he publicly advocated inoculation against smallpox. His *Christian Philosopher* is the first American effort to support Christianity—really the new piety—by arguments drawn from the sciences. Written from premises wholly different from those of the older Puritanism, the book is optimistic and full of expressions of admiration for nature. Mather argues that the whole universe points to God's existence, his wisdom, and his benevolence. Since he leans heavily on the many English works that anticipated his, there is little that is original or important about the book—except that it is a milestone in the history of the decline of Puritanism.[29]

VI   *The Great Awakening and Its Aftermath*

In the church of Northampton, Massachusetts, in the year 1735—not many years after Cotton Mather's death—a remarkable religious revival took place. Jonathan Edwards, its minister, played an important role in the events there and wrote an impressive account soon after. He tells how all of the townsfolk

seemed to be seized with a deep concern about their eternal salvation. All the talk in all companies and upon occasions was upon the things of religion, and no other talk was anywhere relished, and scarcely a single person in the whole town was left unconcerned about the great things of the eternal world. Those that were wont to be the vainest and loosest persons in town seemed in general to be seized with strong convictions. Those that were most disposed to condemn vital and experimental religion and those that had the greatest conceit of their own reason, the highest families in the town and many little children were affected remarkably. No one family that I know of and scarcely a person has been exempt, and the spirit of God went on in his saving influences, to the appearance of all human reason and charity, in a truly wonderful and astonishing manner. [30]

Soon the revival spread to the other places up and down the Connecticut River valley. It lasted only until 1737, but it was the precursor of a much greater revival, the Great Awakening that seized the colonies from New England to Georgia in the 1740s. While many New England ministers who identified themselves with the Puritan tradition welcomed the conversions that added members to the often thin congregations, ultimately the Awakening badly damaged what remained of the fabric of Puritanism.[31]

The Awakening was spread by itinerant ministers, of whom the most notable was George Whitefield, an Anglican who was also a founder of Methodism. These evangelists often addressed not only churches and congregations but crowds in the streets and in the fields. People gathered from many miles to hear. Some itinerants attacked the local minister, especially if he were not a supporter of their activities, declaring sometimes that he had never been converted. Laymen as well as visiting ministers preached, often teaching doctrines that were far from orthodox. One minister noted that "the old divinity, which had stood the test of above seventeen hundred years, is become stale and unsavory to many wanton palates, and nothing will please them but new preachers, new doctrines, new methods of speech, tone, and gesture." The new was destroying the old. Those who were caught up in the enthusiasm often abandoned the Congregational principle that a minister is ordained by his people, who were his distinct responsibility.[32]

Many ministers opposed the disruptions of the Great Awakening. Charles Chauncy of Boston, who wrote the most extended attack, *Seasonable Thoughts on the State of Religion in New England* (1743), saw the revivals as creators of disorder. He denounced those "religious exercises where the churches and ministry are freely declared against by those who have gone out from them, under the pretence of being more holy than they." Some of those who "went out" founded churches apart from the semi-established Congregational ones. Revivalists established colleges to train their own ministers. In sum, there was—in C. C. Goen's words—"a permanent shattering of the Congregational establishment in New England."[33]

One of the two large groups that emerged was the Opposers, or Old Lights, many of whose members—partly in reaction to the enthusiasm and emotionalism of the revivals—favored reason, order, morality. Some of these had already begun to abandon Calvinism in favor of Arminian or some other form of voluntarism. Jonathan Mayhew of Boston, for example, argued that the unregenerate can, by cultivating the means of grace, meet the conditions for receiving God's grace and the regeneration that results from it. Thus while some of the Old Lights remained Old Calvinists, others were the forerunners of Unitarianism. Harvard became more and more the intellectual headquarters of religious liberalism, though it was some years before Harvard became "officially" liberal, with the appointment of Henry Ware as Hollis Professor of Divinity in 1805 and the inauguration of another liberal, John Thornton Kirkland, as president the following year.[34]

Those who supported the Awakening, the New Lights, developed a new theology. Jonathan Edwards, the intellectual leader of the new school—usually called Edwardseans—created a new fabric of thought that brought together the Calvinism of earlier Puritanism and aspects of Enlightenment thought, notably Locke's view of the operation of the human mind. While Edwards was profoundly influenced by the Puritan tradition—he cited Shepard and Hooker in footnotes—his thought is so original that it is misleading to call him a Puritan. He was sympathetic with some older Puritan ideals, such as the restriction of the Lord's Supper to "visible saints." His closest ties to Puritanism are, probably, his devotion to introspection, revealed clearly in his "Personal Narrative," and his profound conviction that man by nature is wholly sinful, a subject he took up in his "The Nature of True Virtue" (1765) and *The Great Christian Doctrine of Original Sin Defended* (1758).[35]

Puritanism decayed because it lost its status as the unique religious force in much of New England, because secularism and religious liberalism (the consequences of the Enlightenment) were able to gain adherents, because Puritanism itself was burdened with contradictions, because its heirs became divided. It did not fall apart like the deacon's "one-hoss shay" in Oliver Wendell Holmes's poem. It did not go to pieces all at once. Puritan concepts and attitudes contributed to the patriotic cause at the time of the American Revolution, especially the belief that America was a new place, ordained by God as the seat of a pure society, uncontaminated by the decadent luxuries of the Old World. Puritanism remained a vital force in America for some one hundred and fifty years. Its inheritors, those who recognized the power of their Puritan ancestry, included such diverse personages as John Adams, Harriet Beecher Stowe, and Ralph Waldo Emerson. The end of the influence of Puritanism has not yet been reached.[36]

Notes and References

Chapter One

1. John Jewel to Peter Martyr at Zurich, in *The Zurich Letters*, ed. Hastings Robinson (Cambridge, Eng., 1852), p. 23. Later Jewel told Martyr with satisfaction, " . . . as to matters of doctrine, we have pared everything to the very quick, and do not differ from your doctrine by a nail's breadth." But he complained about the "vestiges of error," notably the required surplice (p. 100). See also Leonard J. Trinterud, ed., *Elizabethan Puritanism* (New York, 1971), pp. 3 - 7; J. E. Neale, "The Elizabethan Acts of Supremacy and Uniformity," *English Historical Review*, 65 (1950), 304 - 332; Everett H. Emerson, *English Puritanism from John Hooper to John Milton* (Durham, N.C., 1968), pp. 7 - 11; J. H. Primus, *The Vestments Controversy: An Historical Study of the Earliest Tensions Within the Church of England in the Reigns of Edward VI and Elizabeth* (Kampen, Holland, 1960), especially pp. 71 - 106; Horton Davies, *Worship and Theology in England from Cranmer to Hooker* (Princeton, N.J., 1970), pp. 210 - 211; William Clebsch, *England's Earliest Protestants, 1520 - 1535* (New Haven, Conn., 1964).

2. Trinterud, *Elizabethan Puritanism*, pp. 9 - 16, 193 - 197, discusses discriminatingly the first three groups. On the Separatists, see Patrick Collinson, *The Elizabethan Puritan Movement* (Berkeley and Los Angeles, Cal., 1967), pp. 87 - 91, 380 - 382, 388 - 389, and above, pp. 38 - 44. On the development of the practical Puritans, see William Haller, *The Rise of Puritanism* (New York, 1938), and M. M. Knappen, *Tudor Puritanism* (Chicago, 1939).

3. On the problem of definition, see Christopher Hill, "The Definition of a Puritan," in *Society and Puritanism in Pre-Revolutionary England* (London, 1964), and Basil Hall, "Puritanism: The Problem of Definition," in *Studies in Church History*, Volume II, ed. G. J. Cuming (London, 1965).

4. Cartwright, *The Second Replie* (n.p., 1575), pp. 440, 94; *Replye to an Answer* (n.p., 1573), p. 13.

5. *Replye*, pp. 15, 138; *Second Replie*, pp. 59, 61; *The Rest of the Second Replie* (n.p., 1577), pp. 45, 48, 51, 91, 171; John S. Coolidge, *The Pauline Renaissance in England: Puritanism and the Bible* (Oxford, 1970).

6. *A Golden Chaine*, in Perkins, *Workes*, 3 vols. (Cambridge, England, 1608 - 09), I, 78 - 85. On the centrality of the conversion experience, see Gerald C. Brauer, "Reflections on the Nature of English Puritanism," *Church History*, 23 (1954), 99 - 108.

7. *Workes*, I, 362 - 373.

8. *Workes*, I, 728, 732; David Little, *Religion, Law, and Order* (Oxford, 1970), especially pp. 118 - 126; Christopher Hill, *Puritanism and Revolution* (London, 1958), pp. 215 - 238; and Hill, *Society and Puritanism*.

9. Perkins, *The Art of Prophecying*, in *Workes*, II, 732 - 762; Udall, *A Commentarie Upon the Lamentations of Jeremy* (London, 1593), sig. A2 verso; Everett H. Emerson, "John Udall and the Puritan Sermon," *Quarterly Journal of Speech*, 44 (1958), 282 - 284.

10. Lawrence H. Sasek, *The Literary Temper of the English Puritans* (Baton Rouge, La., 1961), pp. 39 - 56.

11. Mather, *Magnalia Christi Americana* (Hartford, Conn., 1853), I, 148.

12. Mather, *Magnalia*, I, 339 - 340; *William Ames by Matthew Nethenus, Hugo Visscher, and Karl Reuter*, trans. Douglas Horton (Cambridge, Mass., 1965); John Eusden's edition of *The Marrow of Theology* (Boston, 1968); and Keith L. Sprunger, *The Learned Doctor William Ames* (Urbana, Ill., 1972). On Ames's influence in America, see Perry Miller, *The New England Mind: The Seventeenth Century* (Cambridge, Mass., 1954; originally published in 1939), p. 48 and passim.

13. Ames, *Marrow*, pp. 77, 80, 159, 171, 177, 180, 226; Visscher, *Ames*, pp. 80 - 81; Reuter, *Ames*, pp. 171, 185 - 191.

14. Ramus, *Commentariorum de Religione Christiana, Libri quator* (Frankfort, 1576), p. 6; Miller, *New England Mind*, pp. 115 - 157; Keith L. Sprunger, "Ames, Ramus, and the Method of Puritan Theology," *Harvard Theological Review*, 59 (1966), 133 - 151. Ames's two logical works are *Demonstratio Logicae Verae* and *Theses Logicae* (both Cambridge, England, 1646). See Wilbur S. Howell, *Logic and Rhetoric in England, 1500 - 1700* (Princeton, N.J., 1956), pp. 210 - 211. On the dichotomies, see Walter J. Ong, *Ramus, Method, and the Decay of Dialogue* (Cambridge, Mass., 1958), pp. 199 - 202.

15. Ames, *Marrow*, pp. 178 - 180; Coolidge, *Pauline Renaissance*, pp. 63 - 71.

16. *Conscience, with the Power and Cases Thereof* (n.p., 1639), Bk. IV, 63, 64.

17. Ames, *Marrow*, pp. 209 - 210; Cotton, *Way of the Congregational Churches* (London, 1648), p. 13. Both Parker and Baynes had died as early as 1617.

18. W. M. Southgate, "The Marian Exiles and the Influence of John Calvin," *History*, 27 (1942), 148 - 152; Charles D. Cremeans, *The Reception of Calvinist Thought in England* (Urbana, Ill., 1949); T. M. Parker, "Arminianism and Laudianism in Seventeenth-Century England," in *Studies in Church History*, Vol. I, eds. C. W. Dugmore and Charles Duggan (London, 1964); W. R. Fryer, "The 'High Churchmen' of the Earlier Seventeenth Century," *Renaissance and Modern Studies*, 5 (1961),

106 - 148; H. G. Alexander, *Religion in England, 1558 - 1662* (London, 1968).

19.   Philip Schaff, ed., *The Creeds of Christendom* (New York, 1877), II, 561 - 597.

20.   Haller, *The Rise of Puritanism*, pp. 89, 168.

21.   *Memoirs of the Life of Colonel Hutchinson*, ed. C. H. Firth (New York, 1885), I, 114 - 115.

22.   Christopher Hill, *Society and Puritanism;* Hugh Trevor-Roper, "James I and his Bishops," *History Today*, 5 (1953), 571 - 581; Alexander, *Religion in England*, pp. 123 - 125, 133 - 135, 144 - 147; Michael Walzer, *The Revolution of the Saints: A Study in the Origins of Radical Politics* (Cambridge, Mass., 1965).

23.   Laud, *Works* (Oxford, 1847 - 60), IV, 60; Paul S. Seaver, *The Puritan Lectureships: The Politics of Religious Dissent, 1560 - 1662* (Stanford, Cal., 1970), especially pp. 240 - 262; Hugh Trevor-Roper, *Archbishop Laud, 1573 - 1645* (London, 1962), pp. 106 - 109, 120 - 121, 151 - 152.

24.   *Articles* (n.p., 1640), pp. 9, 11.

25.   B. E. Supple, *Commercial Crisis and Change in England, 1600 - 1642* (Cambridge, Eng., 1959), pp. 121 - 144.

26.   Louis B. Wright, *The Dream of Prosperity in Colonial America* (New York, 1968); Carl Bridenbaugh, *Vexed and Troubled Englishmen, 1590 - 1642* (New York, 1968), pp. 394 - 410; Everett H. Emerson, *Captain John Smith* (New York, 1971), especially pp. 103 - 118.

27.   David Berkowitz's forthcoming biography of John Selden; Elizabeth Wade White, *Anne Bradstreet, "The Tenth Muse"* (New York, 1971), pp. 79 - 89; John Rushworth, *Historical Collections* (London, 1721), I, 473; Emily C. Williams, *William Coddington of Rhode Island* (Newport, R.I., 1941), p. 5.

28.   "An Epistle Written to the Elders," in Simeon Ashe and William Rathband, *A Letter of Many Ministers* (London, 1643); Bridenbaugh, *Englishmen*, pp. 450 - 457; Everett Emerson, ed., *Letters from New England, 1629 - 1638: The Massachusetts Bay Colony* (Amherst, Mass., 1976).

29.   Bradford, *Of Plymouth Plantation*, ed. Samuel Eliot Morison (New York, 1952), pp. 23 - 25.

30.   Frances Rose-Troup, *The Massachusetts Bay Company and Its Predecessors* (New York, 1930); Samuel Eliot Morison, *Builders of the Bay Colony* (rev. ed., Boston, 1964), pp. 21 - 51.

31.   Alexander Young, ed., *Chronicles of the First Planters of the Colony of Massachusetts Bay* (Boston, 1846), pp. 142, 158, 160; Perry Miller, *Orthodoxy in Massachusetts, 1630 - 1650* (Cambridge, Mass., 1933), especially pp. 129 - 133, 119 - 126; Raymond P. Stearns, *Congregationalism in the Dutch Netherlands* (Chicago, 1940), pp. 1 - 17; Alice C. Carter, *The English Church in Amsterdam in the Seventeenth Century* (Amsterdam, 1964).

32.   Winthrop in *Winthrop Papers*, ed. Allyn B. Forbes and others, 5 vols. to date (Boston, 1929 -   ), II, 114 - 115.

33.   *Winthrop Papers*, III, 338 - 344. See also Daniel B. Shea, *Spiritual Autobiography in Early America* (Princeton, N.J., 1968), pp. 100 - 110; for Culverwell, see Benjamin Brook, *The Lives of the Puritans* (London, 1813), III, 512 - 513.

Chapter Two

1.   Bridenbaugh, *Vexed and Troubled Englishmen*, and Timothy H. Breen and Stephen Foster, "Moving to the New World: The Character of Early Massachusetts Migration," *William and Mary Quarterly*, 3rd Series, 30 (1973), 189 - 222.

2.   Breen and Foster, "Moving to the New World"; Breen, "Persistent Localism: English Social Change and the Shaping of New England Institutions," *William and Mary Quarterly*, 3rd Series, 32 (1975), 3 - 18.

3.   Breen, "Persistent Localism," pp. 18 - 28; Richard Gildrie, *Salem, Massachusetts, 1626 - 1683: A Covenant Community* (Charlottesville, Va., 1975), pp. 39 - 51.

4.   Timothy H. Breen and Stephen Foster, "The Puritans' Greatest Achievement: A Study of Social Cohesion in Seventeenth-Century Massachusetts," *Journal of American History*, 70 (1973 - 74), 5 - 22; Gildrie, *Salem*, p. 35.

5.   See Perry Miller, "Declension in a Bible Commonwealth," in *Nature's Nation* (Cambridge, Mass., 1967) and Robert Pope, "New England Versus the New England Mind: The Myth of Declension," *Journal of Social History*, 3 (1969 - 1970), 301 - 318; Emory Elliott, *Power and the Pulpit in Puritan New England* (Princeton, N.J., 1975).

6.   See the history of Bradford's history in Morison's edition.

7.   Bradford, "A Dialogue," in Alexander Young, ed., *Chronicles of the Pilgrim Fathers* (Boston, 1844), pp. 414 - 470; Browne, *An Answere to Master Cartwright His Letter for Ioyning with the English Churches*, in *The Writings of Robert Harrison and Robert Browne*, ed. Albert Peel and Leland H. Carlson (London, 1953), p. 464; B. R. White, *The English Separatist Tradition, From the Marian Martyrs to the Pilgrim Fathers* (London, 1971). On the uncertain relationship between Separatist and non-Separatist Congregationalism, see Champlin Burrage, *The Early English Dissenters*, 2 vols. (New York, 1967), I, 281 ff., and Perry Miller, *Orthodoxy in Massachusetts* (New York, 1970), p. 73 ff. Since Browne later abandoned Separatism and rejoined the Church of England, later Separatists were careful to deny his influence.

8.   Bradford, *Plymouth Plantation*, pp. 9 - 11. George F. Willison, *Saints and Strangers* (New York, 1945), tells the story of the Pilgrims' English and Continental experience.

9.   George Langdon, *Pilgrim Colony: A History of New Plymouth*,

1620 - 1691 (New Haven, Conn., 1966), pp. 100 - 125; White, *English Separatist Tradition*, pp. 156 - 159.

10.   William Haller, *Foxe's "Book of Martyrs" and the Elect Nation* (London, 1963), p. 208; also published as *The Elect Nation: The Meaning and Relevance of Foxe's "Book of Martyrs"* (New York, 1963); White, *English Separatist Tradition*, pp. 1 - 14; Bradford, "Dialogue," pp. 442 - 443.

11.   Mather, *Magnalia*, I, 25; Bradford, *Plymouth Plantation*, pp. 6, 8; Robert Daly, "William Bradford's Vision of History," *American Literature*, 44 (1973), 557 - 569; Peter Gay, *A Loss of Mastery: Puritan Historians in Colonial America* (Berkeley and Los Angeles, Cal., 1966).

12.   Bradford, *Plymouth Plantation*, pp. 11, 58, 65 - 66, 70, 81.

13.   Ibid., pp. 112, 328, 236, 223 - 224; William Hubbard, *A General History of New England* (Cambridge, Mass., 1815), I, 117; Edward Winslow, *Hypocrisie Unmasked* (London, 1646), p. 92. On Plymouth's influence on Salem, see Langdon, *Plymouth Colony*, pp. 107 - 114; Worthington C. Ford's edition of Bradford's history (Boston, 1912) II, 89 - 95; Miller, *Orthodoxy in Massachusetts*, pp. 128 - 138 and David Hall's preface; Edmund S. Morgan, *Visible Saints: The History of a Puritan Idea* (New York, 1963), pp. 90 - 98. Larzer Ziff argued that it was the "practical success" of the Salem church in defying the Church of England that led religious leaders such as John Cotton to adopt the ways of Salem. See "The Salem Puritans in the 'Free Aire of a New World,' " *Huntington Library Quarterly*, 20 (1957), 380.

14.   Bradford, *Plymouth Plantation*, pp. 252 - 254, 33.

15.   Ibid., pp. 46, 62 - 63; Alan Howard, "Art and History in Bradford's *Of Plymouth Plantation*," *William and Mary Quarterly*, 3rd Series, 28 (1971), 237 - 266.

16.   Bradford, *Plymouth Plantation*, p. 46; Jesper Rosenmeier, "With My Owne Eyes: William Bradford's *Of Plymouth Plantation*," in Sacvan Bercovitch, ed., *Typology and Early American Literature* (Amherst, Mass., 1972).

17.   Dudley, in *Letters from New England*, ed. Emerson, p. 75; Cotton, *Gods Promise to His Plantation* (London, 1630); Winthrop, "Christian Charitie. A Modell Hereof," in *Winthrop Papers*, II, 282 - 295; Shepard, as quoted by Perry Miller, *The New England Mind: The Seventeenth Century* (Cambridge, Mass., 1954; first published 1939), p. 471. I have not been able to locate this last quotation, which Miller identifies as from Shepard's 1638 election sermon. Compare "Thomas Shepard's Election Sermon, in 1638," *New England Historical and Genealogical Register*, 24 (1870), 361 - 366.

18.   The best single source for early Massachusetts history is John Winthrop's journal, of which the best edition is *The History of New England from 1630 to 1649*, ed. James Savage (Boston, 1853); David D. Hall, *The Faithful Shepherd: A History of the New England Ministry in*

the Seventeenth Century (Chapel Hill, N.C., 1972); Babette May Levy, *Preaching in the First Half-Century of New England History* (Hartford, Conn., 1945), pp. 1 - 12.

19. Hubbard, *A General History of New England* (Boston, 1878), p. 181; Hall, *Faithful Shepherd*, pp. 72 - 88; Miller, *Orthodoxy*, pp. 119 - 149; Norman Pettit, "Hooker's Doctrine of Assurance: A Critical Phase in New England Spiritual Thought," *New England Quarterly*, 47 (1974), 518 - 534.

20. *A Platform of Church Discipline* in *The Creeds and Platforms of Congregationalism*, ed. Williston Walker (New York, 1893), pp. 207 - 218; Emil Oberholzer, *Delinquent Saints: Disciplinary Acts in the Early Congregational Churches of Massachusetts* (New York, 1956); Thomas Lechford, *Plain Dealing, or News from New England* (1642), ed. J. Hammond Trumbull (New York, 1969), pp. 29 - 31.

21. Larzer Ziff, "The Social Bond of Church Covenant," *American Quarterly*, 10 (1958), 454 - 462.

22. Cotton, *A Coppy of a Letter of Mr. John Cotton* (n.p., 1641), pp. 5 - 6; Morgan, *Visible Saints*, pp. 8 - 112.

23. Two of these works, *The Keyes* and *The Way Cleared*, have been edited in a modernized form as *John Cotton on the Churches of New England*, ed. Larzer Ziff (Cambridge, Mass., 1968).

24. Cotton, *Way of the Churches*, pp. 3 - 4; Winthrop, *Winthrop Papers*, IV, 170.

25. Cotton, *Way of the Churches*, pp. 6 - 7; on the relationship of church and state, see Edwin Powers, *Crime and Punishment in Early Massachusetts, 1620 - 1692* (Boston, 1966), pp. 100 - 162.

26. Richard D. Pearce, ed., *The Records of the First Church in Boston, 1630 - 1868* in *Publications* of the Colonial Society of Massachusetts, 39 (1961), 12.

27. Samuel G. Drake, *History of Boston* (Boston, 1856), pp. 310 - 311; *The Records of the Governor and Company of the Massachusetts Bay*, ed. N. B. Shurtleff (Boston, 1853 - 54), I, 87.

28. Cudworth in *Letters from New England*, ed. Emerson, p. 141

29. Walker, *Creeds and Platforms*, pp. 235 - 236; *Book of the General Lawes and Libertyes of Massachusetts*, ed. Thomas G. Barnes (San Marino, Cal., 1975); see also John Cotton's 1648 letter in *Winthrop Papers*, V, 192 - 193, and Edmund S. Morgan, ed., *Puritan Political Theory* (Indianapolis, Ind., 1965).

30. Cotton, letter to Lord Say and Seal, 1636, in *Letters from New England*, ed. Emerson, p. 191; answers to Lord Say and Seal and others by "leading men," in Thomas Hutchinson, *The History of the Colony and Province of Massachusetts Bay*, ed. Lawrence Shaw Mayo, 3 vols. (Cambridge, Mass., 1936), I, 412 - 413; Shepard, "Election Sermon," p. 366.

31. *Winthrop Papers*, IV, 170; Edmund S. Morgan, *The Puritan Dilemma: The Story of John Winthrop* (Boston, 1958), pp. 84 - 100; *Hutchinson*

Papers (Albany, N.Y., 1865), I, 79 - 80; John D. Eusden, "Natural Law and Covenant Theology in New England, 1620 - 1670," *Natural Law Forum*, 6 (1960), 9.

32. Cotton, *The Way Cleared*, p. 102. Also see Cotton's *The Powrring out of the Seven Vials* (London, 1642) and *The Churches Resurrection* (London, 1642), and Joy B. Gilsdorf, "The Puritan Apocalypse: New England Eschatology in the Seventeenth Century," unpublished Ph.D. dissertation, Yale, 1964, pp. 138 - 143.

33. J. F. Maclear, "New England and the Fifth Monarchy: The Quest for the Millenium in Early American Puritanism," *William and Mary Quarterly*, 3rd Series, 32 (1976), 223 - 225.

34. Quoted from Harrison T. Meserole, ed., *Seventeenth-Century American Poetry* (Garden City, N.Y., 1968), pp. 397 - 398.

35. Everett Emerson, *John Cotton* (New York, 1965), pp. 95 - 101; Edward Johnson, *History* (London, 1654), p. 32.

36. Johnson, *History*, p. 34; *Winthrop Papers*, V, 126.

37. Maclear, "New England and the Fifth Monarchy," pp. 257 - 259.

38. Winthrop, *Winthrop Papers*, II, 294; Hall, *Faithful Shepherd*, pp. 121 - 155; Cotton, *The Way Cleared*, p. 102; Darrett B. Rutman, *Winthrop's Boston: Portrait of a Puritan Town, 1630 - 1649* (Chapel Hill, N.C., 1965), p. 146. "Profane and debauched persons" were not permitted to reside in the colony. See Thomas Dudley's letter in *Letters from New England*, ed. Emerson, p. 75.

39. Ernst Troeltsch, *The Social Teachings of the Christian Churches*, trans. Olive Wyon (New York, 1949), I, 331. The relevance of Troeltsch's model was suggested to me by Robert G. Pope, *The Half-Way Covenant: Church Membership in Puritan New England* (Princeton, N.J., 1969), pp. 261 - 262.

40. Calvin, *Commentaries on Genesis* (Edinburgh, 1847), I, 444; Calvin, *Institutes*, ed. John T. McNeill (Philadelphia, 1960), I, 429, 450, 808; Everett H. Emerson, "Calvin and Covenant Theology," *Church History*, 25 (1956), 136 - 144; Jens G. Møller, "The Beginnings of Puritan Covenant Theology," *Journal of Ecclesiastical History*, 14 (1963), 46 - 50; Leonard J. Trinterud, ed., *Elizabethan Puritanism* (New York, 1971), pp. 307 - 308.

41. Michael McGiffert, "The Problem of the Covenant in Puritan Thought: Peter Bulkeley's Gospel-Covenant," *New England Historical and Genealogical Register*, 130 (1976), 107 - 129. The fullest and most famous discussion of Puritan covenant theology is Perry Miller's "The Marrow of Puritan Divinity" (1935), reprinted in *Errand into the Wilderness* (Cambridge, Mass., 1956). Miller's treatment has been frequently challenged. See Michael McGiffert's survey, "American Puritan Studies in the 1960's," *William and Mary Quarterly*, 3rd Series, 27 (1970), 36 - 67; George M. Marsden, "Perry Miller's Rehabilitation of the Puritans: A Critique,"

Church History, 39 (1970), 91 - 105; and Robert Middlekauf's essay on Miller in Pastmasters: Some Essays on American Historians, ed. Marcus Cunliffe and Robin Wicks (New York, 1969).

42. Bulkeley, The Gospel-Covenant, or the Covenant of Grace Opened, second edition (London, 1651), pp. 313, 319.

43. Ibid., pp. 426 - 429. On the troublesome distinction, see Coolidge, Pauline Renaissance in England, p. 109 ff.

44. Bulkeley, Gospel-Covenant, pp. 104 - 105; Westminster Confession, Chapters X and XV.

45. Hooker, The Christians Two Chiefe Lessons (London, 1640), p. 218; The Application of Redemption, The Ninth and Tenth Books (London, 1659), p. 206; Four Treatises (London, 1638), p. 252; The Saints Dignitie, and Dutie (London, 1651), pp. 240 - 241.

46. Shepard, Certain Select Cases Resolved (London, 1650), pp. 16 -17. Jonathan Edwards, who frequently cited Shepard's works, made a similar distinction and found that involuntary sin, sin by nature, is much the worse kind. See Edwards, A Treatise Concerning Religious Affections, ed. John E. Smith (New Haven, Conn., 1959).

47. Shepard, Subjection to Christ in All His Ordiances and Appointments (London, 1652), p. 152 and passim; Shepard, The Parable of the Ten Virgins Opened and Applied (London, 1660); Jesper Rosenmeier, "New England's Perfection: The Image of Adam and the Image of Christ in the Antinomian Crisis, 1634 to 1638," William and Mary Quarterly, 3rd Series, 27 (1970), especially 445.

48. Bulkeley, Gospel-Covenant, p. 23; Creeds and Platforms, ed. Walker, p. 206; Hooker, Covenant of Grace (London, 1649), pp. 35 - 36.

49. Hooker, Covenant of Grace, pp. 16 - 21. See also E. Brooks Holifield, The Covenant Sealed: The Development of Puritan Sacramental Theology (New Haven, Conn., 1974).

50. Winthrop, History, I, 144; Hall, Faithful Shepherd, pp. 156 - 158, 162 - 166.

51. Alden Vaughan, New England Frontier: Puritans and Indians, 1620 - 1675 (Boston, Massachusetts, 1965), pp. 235 - 263; Francis Jennings, The Invasion of America: Indians, Colonialism and the Cant of Conquest (Chapel Hill, N.C., 1975).

Chapter Three

1. Winthrop, History, ed. Savage, I, 63.

2. Ola E. Winslow, Master Roger Williams (New York, 1957); Edmund S. Morgan, Roger Williams: The Church and the State (New York, 1967).

3. Edward Trelawny in Letters from New England, ed. Emerson, pp. 176 - 177; Williams, Complete Writings, 7 vols. (New York, 1963), IV, 271; V, 103.

4. Williams, *Complete Writings*, IV, 336; VII, 32 - 41; II, 272; I, 389; III, 234, 290. Winthrop, *History*, I, 194.

5. Hall, *Faithful Shepherd*, pp. 121 - 155.

6. Cotton, "How Far Moses Judicialls Bind Massachusetts," in Worthington C. Ford, "Cotton's 'Moses His Judicials,' " in *Proceedings* of the Massachusetts Historical Society, 2nd Series, 16 (1903), 281, 284 (the second passage was reconstructed by Ford); Cotton, *Bloudy Tenent, Washed* (London, 1647), pp. 126 and 92; Sacvan Bercovitch, "Typology in Puritan New England: The Williams-Cotton Controversy Reassessed," *American Quarterly*, 19 (1967), 166 - 191.

7. Williams, *Complete Writings*, III, 303, 104; Jesper Rosenmeier, "The Teacher and the Witness: John Cotton and Roger Williams," *William and Mary Quarterly*, 3rd Series, 25 (1968), 408 - 431.

8. Cotton, "Letter to Lord Say and Seal," in *Letters from New England*, ed. Emerson, p. 191; Cotton, *Bloudy Tenent Washed*, p. 68; Winthrop, *History*, II, 280; Williams, *Complete Writings*, IV, 187.

9. Williams, *Complete Writings*, IV, 186 - 188; III, 331, 398.

10. Ibid., VII, 159; III, 250.

11. Ibid., I, 342; IV, 243. Hooker agreed with Cotton. See "A Thomas Hooker Sermon of 1638," *Resources for American Literary Study*, 2 (1972), 81.

12. Perry Miller, *The New England Mind: From Colony to Province* (Cambridge, Mass., 1953), pp. 21 - 22: Williams, *Complete Writings*, IV, 209; Emil Oberholzer, *Delinquent Saints: Disciplinary Action in the Early Congregational Churches of Massachusetts* (New York, 1956).

13. Cotton, *The Controversie Concerning Liberty of Conscience* (London, 1649), p. 7; Williams, *Complete Writings*, III, 272.

14. Arthur H. Buffington, "The Massachusetts Experiment of 1630," *Publications* of the Colonial Society of Massachusetts, 32 (1933 - 37), 308 - 320; Emerson, introduction to *Letters from New England*.

15. Emery Battis, *Saints and Sectaries: Anne Hutchinson and the Antinomian Controversy in the Massachusetts Bay Colony* (Chapel Hill, N.C., 1962); David D. Hall, ed., *The Antinomian Controversy, 1636 - 1638; A Documentary History* (Middletown, Conn., 1968); Hall, *Faithful Shepherd*, pp. 159 - 162; Jesper Rosenmeier, "New England's Perfection: The Image of Adam and the Image of Christ in the Antinomian Crisis, 1634 to 1638," *William and Mary Quarterly*, 3rd Series, 27 (1970), 435 - 459; Edmund S. Morgan's chapter "Seventeenth-Century Nihilism," in his *Puritan Dilemma;* Norman Pettit, *The Heart Prepared: Grace and Conversion in Puritan Spiritual Life* (New Haven, Conn., 1966); Darrett Rutman, *Winthrop's Boston, a Portrait of a Puritan Town 1630 - 1649* (Chapel Hill, N.C., 1965), pp. 111 - 126; Emerson, *John Cotton*, pp. 112 - 125.

16. The best description of the sense of excitement is probably Edward Johnson's, in his *History of New-England* (London, 1654).

17. *Parable of the Ten Virgins* (London, 1660), Pt.I, pp. 174, 175.

18.   Cotton, "Rejoynder," in *Antinomian Controversy*, pp. 101 - 102, 104.

19.   Shepard, *The Sound Beleever* (London, 1652), p. 246; Pettit, *Heart Prepared*, pp. 108 - 114.

20.   Cotton, *A Treatise of the Covenant of Grace* (London, 1659), pp. 39 - 40, 65 - 66.

21.   Cotton, *The Way Cleared*, p. 51; Battis, *Saints and Sectaries*.

22.   Winthrop, *History*, I, 240 - 264; Wheelwright, "Fast-Day Sermon" in Charles H. Bell, *John Wheelwright, His Writings* (Boston, 1876), p. 161; Winthrop, *A Short Story*, in *Antinomian Controversy*, p. 203.

23.   Cotton, *Treatise of the Covenant*, p. 21; Winthrop, *A Short Story*, in *Antinomian Controversy*, p. 274.

24.   Clapp, "Memoirs," in *Chronicles of the First Planters*, ed. Young, p. 355; Johnson, *History of New England*, pp. 95 - 96; James F. Maclear, " 'The Heart of New England Rent': The Mystical Element in Early Puritan History," *Mississippi Valley Historical Review*, 47, (1956), 621 - 652.

25.   Dudley, in the General Court's examination of Mrs. Hutchinson, *Antinomian Controversy*, pp. 317 - 318; Cotton, *Bloudy Tenent Washed*, Pt. II, p. 51. Hutchinson, *History of Massachusetts Bay*, ed. Mayo, I, 58.

26.   Winthrop, *Short Story*, in *Antinomian Controversy*, p. 209; Hall, in *Antinomian Controversy*, pp. 9, 20; Charles F. Adams, *Massachusetts, Its History and Its Historians* (Boston, 1893).

27.   James W. Jones, *The Shattered Synthesis: New England Puritanism before the Great Awakening* (New Haven, Conn., 1973), pp. 3 - 31; McGiffert, "Problem of the Covenant," pp. 107 - 129.

28.   Williston Walker, ed., *The Creeds and Platforms of Congregationalism* (New York, 1893), pp. 141, 137, 159 - 165. A version of the incident discussed below appears in Robert Emmet Wall, Jr., *Massachusetts Bay: The Critical Decade, 1640 - 1650* (New Haven, Conn., 1972). The approved version of Hooker's survey was lost at sea; the published version is a reconstruction.

29.   Walker, *Creeds*, pp. 164 - 165. An unpublished treatise, "A Model of Civil and Church Power," composed in 1635 or 1636, explains "how the civil state and the church may dispense their several governments without infringement and impeachment of the power and honor of the one or of the other." Roger Williams quotes from this work, "framed by many able, learned and godly hands," ministers of the Massachusetts Bay colony. See his *Complete Writings*, III, vi - ix, 221 - 222, and Robert F. Scholz, "Clerical Consociation in Massachusetts Bay: Reassessing the New England Way and Its Origins," *William and Mary Quarterly*, 3rd Series, 29 (1972), 391 - 414.

30.   Bernard Bailyn, *The New England Merchants in the Seventeenth Century* (Cambridge, Mass., 1955), p. 107; Wall, *Massachusetts Bay*, pp. 157 - 174.

31.   Walker, *Creeds*, pp. 168 - 171.

32. Ibid., 171 ff.; Winthrop, *History*, II, 389; Perry Miller, "The Cambridge Platform in 1648," in *The Cambridge Platform of 1648*, ed. Henry W. Foote (Boston, 1949).

33. Walker, *Creeds*, pp. 235 - 237.

34. Wall, *Massachusetts Bay*, p. 228.

Chapter Four

1. Stoughton, *New-Englands True Interest* (Cambridge, Mass., 1690), p. 19.

2. *Records of Massachusetts Bay*, IV, Pt.1, p. 367; Morison, *Builders of the Bay Colony*, p. 269; Henry M. Burt, *First Century of the History of Springfield*, 2 vols. (Springfield, Mass.; 1898 - 99), II, 627; Emory Elliott, *Power and the Pulpit*, pp. 16 - 31.

3. John M. Murrin, "Essay Review," *History and Theory*, ll (1972), 236; Morgan, *Visible Saints*, p. 128; Morgan, "New England Puritanism: Another Approach," *William and Mary Quarterly*, 3rd Series, 18 (1961), 236 - 242.

4. Morgan, *Puritan Dilemma*, pp. 84 - 100; Morgan, *Visible Saints*, pp. 100 - 101; B. Katherine Brown, "The Controversy over the Franchise in Puritan Massachusetts, 1954 - 1974," *William and Mary Quarterly*, 3rd Series, 33 (1976), 228 - 233.

5. Cotton, *The Way of Congregational Churches Cleared* (London, 1648), pp. 69 - 73.

6. John Cotton, *Milk for Babes*, a catechism, in Emerson, *John Cotton*, p. 130; Richard Mather, *Church-Government and Church Covenant Discussed* (London, 1643), p. 12; Walker, ed., *Creeds and Platforms of Congregationalism*, p. 224; Holifield, *Covenant Sealed*, pp. 139 - 155.

7. John Cotton, *The Grounds and Ends of the Baptisms of the Children of the Faithful* (London, 1647), p. 137; Holifield, *Covenant Sealed*, pp. 139 - 159.

8. Mitchell in Richard Mather, *A Defence of the Answer* (Cambridge, Mass., 1649), p. 45; Pope, *Half-Way Covenant*, p. 5.

9. Walker, *Creeds*, pp. 328, 331; emphasis provided.

10. Ibid., pp. 278 - 279; Pope, *Half-Way Covenant*, pp. 26 - 57.

11. Walker, *Creeds*, p. 435; Cotton Mather, *A Companion for Communicants* (Boston, 1690), p. 78; Holifield, *Covenant Sealed*, pp. 176 - 178, 186 - 193, 226; Hall, *Faithful Shepherd*, p. 206.

12. Mather, *A Sermon Exhortation to the Present and Succeeding Generation in New England* (Cambridge, Mass., 1671), p. 7; Sacvan Bercovitch, "Horologicals to Chronometricals: The Rhetoric of the Jeremiad," *Literary Monographs*, Vol. III (Madison, 1970).

13. Mather, *A Discourse Concerning the Danger of Apostasy* (Boston, 1679), p. 56; Oakes, *New England Pleaded With* (Cambridge, 1673), p. 23; Robert Middlekauf, *The Mathers: Three Generations of Puritan Intellec-*

tuals, 1596 - 1728 (New York, 1971), especially Chapter 6, "The Invention of New England."

14. Perry Miller, *Nature's Nation* (Cambridge, Mass., 1967), pp. 23 -24.

15. A. W. Plumstead, ed., *The Wall and the Garden: Selected Massachusetts Election Sermons, 1670 - 1775* (Minneapolis, 1968), p. 61; Miller, "Errand into the Wilderness," in Miller, *Errand into the Wilderness* (New York, 1964).

16. Scottow, *A Narrative of the Planting of the Massachusetts Colony* (Boston, 1694), pp. 40 - 41.

17. (London, 1705; first edition Dublin, 1683). I use the reprint prepared by Mason I. Lowance, Jr. (New York, 1969). The quotation is from page 52.

18. Mason I. Lowance, Jr., *Increase Mather* (Boston, 1974), pp. 150 - 151.

19. Hall, *Faithful Shepherd*, pp. 238 - 239.

20. Stoughton, *New Englands True Interest*, in Perry Miller and Thomas H. Johnson, eds., *The Puritans*, 2 vols. (New York, 1963), I, 245; Miller, *The New England Mind: From Colony to Province* (Cambridge, Mass., 1953), p. 33.

21. Oxenbridge, *New England Freemen Warned and Warmed, To Be Free Indeed* (Cambridge, Mass., 1673), pp. 21 - 22; Cotton, *An Exposition upon the Thirteenth Chapter of the Revelation* (London, 1655), p. 77.

22. Sargent Bush, "Thomas Hooker and the Westminster Assembly," *William and Mary Quarterly*, 3rd Series, 29 (1972), 294; Robert S. Paul, ed., *An Apologeticall Narration* (Philadelphia, 1963), pp. 46, 51 - 52, 110 - 112; Gerald R. Cragg, *Puritanism in the Period of the Great Persecution* (Cambridge, Eng., 1957).

23. Minter, "The Puritan Jeremiad as a Literary Form," in Bercovitch, ed., *American Puritan Imagination*, pp. 47, 52; Minter's essay forms part of his book *The Interpreted Design as a Structural Principle in American Prose* (New Haven, Conn., 1969). Gustave Blanke, "Die Anfange des amerikanischer Sendungsbewuststeins, Massachusetts Bay, 1629 bis 1659," *Archiv für Reformationsgeschichte*, 58 (1967), 17 - 211, and J. F. Maclear, "New England and the Fifth Monarchy," pp. 233 - 260. On the later influence of the idea of mission, see Ernest Tuveson, *Redeemer Nation: The Idea of America's Millennial Role* (Chicago, 1968), and Sacvan Bercovitch, *Puritan Origins of the American Self* (New Haven, Conn., 1975).

Chapter Five

1. Ebenezer Hazard, ed., *Historical Collections*, 2 vols. (Philadelphia, 1792 - 94), I, 1 - 6; edition of *First Fruits* in Samuel Eliot Morison, *The Founding of Harvard College* (Cambridge, Mass., 1935), p. 441. Other parts of New England, such as Rhode Island and New Hampshire, had no instituted government and so could not have joined the United Colonies.

John Winthrop made clear that they would not have been welcome to join "because they ran a different course from us, both in their ministry and civil administration"—*History of New England*, ed. Savage, II, 101.

2. See Frank Shuffleton, *Light of the Western Churches: The Career of Thomas Hooker, 1586 - 1647* (Princeton, N.J., 1977), and George H. Williams and others, eds., Thomas Hooker: *Writings in England and Holland, 1626 - 1633* (Cambridge, Mass., 1975).

3. Hooker, *The Christians Two Chiefe Lessons* (London, 1640), pp. 205, 212 and passim; Norman S. Grabo, "The Art of Puritan Devotion," *Seventeenth-Century News*, 26 (1968), 7 - 9.

4. *The Paterne of Perfection* (London, 1640), pp. 5, 19 - 20; *The Soules Exaltation* (London, 1638), pp. 135 - 136.

5. *Paterne*, pp. 54 - 55, 137, 149 - 150, 182, 202; *The Saints Dignitie, and Dutie* (London, 1651), p. 28.

6. *Paterne*, pp. 54, 160; *The Application of Redemption*, Bks. I-VIII (London, 1656), pp. 307 - 313, 318 - 319; *The Application of Redemption*, Bks. IX-X (London, 1657), pp. 254 - 259; *The Unbeleevers Preparing for Christ* (London, 1638), Pt. I, p. 100.

7. *An Exposition of the Principles of Religion* (London, 1645), p. 13; *Soules Exaltation*, pp. 132, 135 - 137, 175; *Application*, Bks. I - VIII, pp. 15 - 19.

8. *Soules Exaltation*, pp. 170 - 171; *The Soules Implantation* (London, 1637), p. 83; *The Soules Vocation* (London, 1638), pp. 33, 283 - 284; *Unbeleevers Preparing*, Pt. I, pp. 32 - 33, Pt. II, pp. 20 - 21, 24.

9. *Application*, Bks. I-VIII, pp. 79, 355 - 367.

10. *A Comment Upon Christ's Last Prayer* (London, 1656), pp. 89 - 90; *The Saints Dignitie*, p. 62.

11. *Soules Vocation*, p. 45; *Application*, Bks. IX-X, pp. 283, 436; *Unbeleevers Preparing*, Pt. I, p. 125; *Application*, Bks. I-VIII, pp. 111, 199; *Saints Dignitie*, pp. 213 - 214.

12. *Application*, Bks. IX-X, p. 29.

13. *Application*, Bks. IX-X, p. 6; *Soules Implantation*, p. 264; *Christians Two Lessons*, p. 62. Self-examination is fully treated in both of the latter two works. See also Norman Pettit, "Hooker's Doctrine of Assurance."

14. *Application*, Bks. IX-X, p. 534 (misnumbered 634); Hubert R. Pellman, "Thomas Hooker: A Study of Puritan Ideals," unpublished Ph.D. dissertation, University of Pennsylvania, 1958; Diane M. Darrow, "Thomas Hooker and the Puritan Art of Preaching," unpublished Ph.D. dissertation, University of California, San Diego, 1968.

15. Mather, *Magnalia*, II, 9; Morison, *Builders of the Bay Colony*, p. 184.

16. Morison, *Founding of Harvard*, p. 432.

17. *Massachusetts Records*, I, 183, 208, 228; Morison, *Founding of Harvard*, p. 169; Johnson, *A History of New England*, p. 164.

18. E. S. Shuckburgh, *Emmanuel College* (London, 1904), p. 23,

quoting Sir Walter Mildmay, the founder. See also Winthrop S. Hudson, "The Morison Myth Concerning the Founding of Harvard," *Church History*, 8 (1939), 149 - 156; Morison, *Founding of Harvard*, pp. 92 - 93, 210 - 223, 264.

19.   Morison, *Founding of Harvard*, pp. 235, 242.

20.   Ibid., p. 433; Hall, *Faithful Shepherd*, pp. 176 - 177.

21.   Charles Chauncey, *Gods Mercy shewed to his people in giving them a faithful Minister and Schooles of Learning* (Cambridge, Mass., 1655), p. 38; S. E. Morison, *Harvard College in the Seventeenth Century*, 2 vols. (Cambridge, Mass., 1936), I, 139 - 145, 267 - 271. Morison quotes Increase Mather at I, 167.

22.   Hall, *Faithful Shepherd*, p. 178; Morison, *Harvard in the Seventeenth Century*, I, 272 - 280; Thomas H. Johnson, ed., *The Poetical Works of Edward Taylor* (Princeton, N. J., 1943), pp. 201 - 220.

23.   Hall, *Faithful Shepherd*, pp. 180 - 181, 185; Lowance, *Increase Mather*, p. 28.

24.   See Sasek, *Literary Temper of the English Puritans*.

25.   I use the text of Kenneth Silverman, ed., *Colonial American Poetry* (New York, 1968). See also his remarks, pp. 31 - 38, 121 - 129, and William J. Scheick, "Standing in the Gap: Urian Oakes' Elegy on Thomas Shepard," *Early American Literature*, 9 (1974 - 75), 301 - 306.

26.   Elizabeth Wade White, *Anne Bradstreet: The Tenth Muse* (New York, 1971); and Ann Stanford, *Anne Bradstreet: The Worldly Puritan: An Introduction to Her Poetry* (New York, 1974).

27.   White, *Bradstreet*, pp. 39 - 41, 43 - 69, 102 ff.

28.   I use the text of *The Works of Anne Bradstreet*, ed. Jeannine Hensley (Cambridge, Mass., 1967).

29.   Ibid., p. 279; Robert D. Richardson, Jr., "The Puritan Poetry of Anne Bradstreet," in *The American Puritan Imagination*, ed. Sacvan Bercovitch (New York, 1974), pp. 107 - 122, first printed in *Texas Studies in Language and Literature*, 9 (1967), 317 - 331.

30.   Alvin H. Rosenfeld, "Anne Bradstreet's 'Contemplations,' " *New England Quarterly*, 43 (1970), 79 - 96; William Irvin, "Allegory and Typology 'Imbrace and Greet': Anne Bradstreet's 'Contemplations,' ", *Early American Literature*, 10 (1975), 30 - 46.

31.   See Constance Gefvert, *Edward Taylor: An Annotated Bibliography, 1668 - 1970* (Kent, Ohio, 1971); Donald E. Stanford, "Edward Taylor and the Lord's Supper," *American Literature*, 27 (1955), 172 - 178; Evan Prosser, "Edward Taylor's Poetry," *New England Quarterly*, 30 (1967), 375 - 398; Thomas M. Davis, "Edward Taylor and the Traditions of Puritan Typology," *Early American Literature*, 4 (1969 - 70), 27 - 47.

32.   Karl Keller, *The Example of Edward Taylor* (Amherst, Mass., 1975), pp. 16 - 24, 34 - 35.

33.   William B. Goodman, "Edward Taylor Writes His Love," *New England Quarterly*, 27 (1954), 510 - 515; Taylor, "A Funerall Poem," in

The Poems of Edward Taylor, ed. Donald E. Stanford (New Haven, Conn., 1960), p. 472; I use this text throughout; Keller, *Taylor,* pp. 43 - 48.

34. See Donald E. Stanford, "Edward Taylor," in *Major Writers of Early American Literature,* ed. Everett Emerson (Madison, Wisconsin, 1972).

35. Taylor, *Poems,* pp. 387, 73, 339; Keller, *Taylor,* pp. 163 - 188; Thomas M. Davis, "Edward Taylor's 'Occasional Meditations,' " *Early American Literature,* 5, (1970 - 71), 17 - 29; James Bray, "John Fiske: Puritan Precursor of Edward Taylor," *Early American Literature,* 9 (1973 - 74), 27 - 38; *God's Plot . . . The Autobiography & Journal of Thomas Shepard,* ed. Michael McGiffert (Amherst, Mass., 1972); and Edmund S. Morgan, *The Puritan Family* (New York, 1966), 161 - 168.

36. On typology, see above, pp. 90 - 92.

37. Taylor, *Poems,* pp. 322, 30, 233, 78, 192, 279; Keller, *Taylor,* pp. 191 - 206.

Chapter Six

1. Hall, *Faithful Shepherd,* pp. 168 - 169; Thomas Lechford, *Plain Dealing, or Newes from New-England,* ed. J. Hammond Trumbull (New York, 1970, originally publ. 1642), p. 43ff; *The Book of the General Lawes,* ed. Thomas G. Barnes (San Marino, Cal., 1975), p. 20.

2. Hooker, *The Soules Preparation for Christ* (London, 1632), p. 83 and passim; Bolton, *Some General Directions for a Comfortable Walking with God* (London, 1625), pp. 25 - 26. See also Norman S. Grabo, "The Art of Puritan Devotion," *Seventeenth-Century News,* 26 (1968), 7 - 9.

3. Hooker, *The Christians Two Chiefe Lessons* (London, 1640), pp. 104, 105 (misnumbered 204, 205).

4. Shepard, *The Parable of the Ten Virgins,* in *Works,* 3 vols., ed. John T. Albro (New York, 1967), II, 632.

5. Cynthia Griffin Wolff, "Literary Reflections of the Puritan Character," *Journal of the History of Ideas,* 29 (1968), 16 - 17; Kenneth B. Murdock, *Literature and Theology in Colonial New England* (New York, 1963), pp. 100 - 104.

6. Shepard, *God's Plot,* ed. McGiffert, pp. 135 - 136.

7. Ibid., pp. 153, 131, 133, 136, 237.

8. Ibid., p. 228.

9. Winthrop in Hall, ed., *Antinomian Controversy,* pp. 341, 342; Shepard, *God's Plot,* p. 229.

10. *The Diary of Michael Wigglesworth, 1653 - 1657: The Conscience of a Puritan,* ed. Edmund S. Morgan (New York, 1965), p. ix.

11. Ibid., pp. 27, 28, 71, 77.

12. Ibid., pp. 29, 58, 53, 61.

13. Ibid., pp. 78, 81, 56, 70.

14. Ibid., pp. 14, 57, 50.

15. Ibid., pp. 3, 4, 79. Steven Kagle's essay on Wigglesworth, part of his forthcoming book on American diaries, was made available to me in manuscript.

16. Sewall, *Diary, 1674 - 1729*, 2 vols., ed. M. Halsey Thomas (New York, 1973), p. 524; Richard Crowder, *No Featherbed to Heaven: A Biography of Michael Wigglesworth, 1631 - 1705* (East Lansing, Mich., 1968).

17. Ola E. Winslow, *Samuel Sewall of Boston* (New York, 1964).

18. *Diary*, p. 367.

19. Ibid., pp. 189, 227, 543, 950 - 951. Sewall published *Phaenomena Quaedam Apocalyptica* (Boston, 1697) and *Proposals Touching the Accomplishments of Prophecies* (Boston, 1713).

20. Cotton Mather, quoted by David E. Stannard, "Death and Dying in Puritan New England," *American Historical Review*, 78 (1973), 1315. See also Stannard's forthcoming book on Puritans and death, a portion of which I saw in manuscript.

21. Robert Middlekauf, "Piety and Intellect in Puritanism," *William and Mary Quarterly*, 3rd Series, 22 (1965), 467 - 470; Alice Morse Earle, *Custom and Fashions in Old New England* (New York, 1893), pp. 374 -376; Dickran and Ann Tashjian, *Memorials for Children of Change: The Art of Early New England Stonecarving* (Middletown, Conn., 1974).

22. *Diary of Cotton Mather (1681 - 1724)*, 2 vols., ed. Worthington C. Ford (New York, 1957), and *The Diary of Cotton Mather, D.D., F.R.S., for the Year 1712*, ed. William R. Manierre, II (Charlottesville, Va., 1964); Sacvan Bercovitch, "Cotton Mather," in *Major Writers*, ed. Emerson; Maclear, " 'The Heart of New-England Rent,' " 621 - 652; Maclear, "New England and the Fifth Monarchy"; Kenneth Silverman, ed., *Selected Letters of Cotton Mather* (Baton Rouge, La., 1971), pp. x - xiii, 88 - 93, 341 - 342; Cotton Mather, *Bonifacius*, ed. David Levin (Cambridge, Mass., 1966), pp. ix - xv.

23. *Diary*, ed. Ford, II, 41, 42, 346, 266.

24. Ibid., II, 47; I, 448, 256.

25. Ibid., I, 253, 254.

26. Ibid., I, 428, 560.

27. Ibid., I, 454, 376, 399 - 400, 404, 409, 411, 419, 455; Miller, *From Colony to Province*, p. 403.

28. *Diary*, II, 705 - 708; Bercovitch, "Cotton Mather," pp. 96 - 105.

29. Bercovitch, *Puritan Origins of the American Self*, pp. 18, 20.

30. David H. Flaherty, *Privacy in Colonial New England* (Charlottesville, Va., 1972), pp. 175 - 179.

Chapter Seven

1. Ward, *The Simple Cobler of Aggawam in America* (London, 1647), p. 3; *Massachusetts Records*, IV, part 1, p. 328.

2. *Massachusetts Records*, IV, part 1, p. 278; William G. McLoughlin, *New England Dissent, 1630 - 1833*, 2 vols. (Cambridge, Mass., 1971), I,

18 - 21. Rufus M. Jones, *The Quakers in the American Colonies* (London, 1911), pp. 26 - 41, 65 - 110.

3. Rhode Island Historical Society *Collections*, 4 (1838), 230; Sidney Ahlstrom, *A Religious History of the American People* (New Haven, Conn., 1972), pp. 166 - 183.

4. Richard Bushman, *From Puritan to Yankee: Character and the Social Order in Connecticut, 1640 - 1765* (Cambridge, Mass., 1967); *Calendar of State Papers, Colonial Series: America and the West Indies, 1661 - 1668* (London, 1880), pp. 8 - 10.

5. *Collection of Original Papers Relative to . . . Massachusetts Bay*, ed. Thomas Hutchinson, 2 vols. (Albany, 1865), II, 101 - 103; *Massachusetts Records*, IV, part 2, p. 169; John G. Palfrey, *History of New England*, 5 vols. (Boston, 1858 - 1890), II, 527.

6. *Massachusetts Records*, V, 346 - 347; Hall, *Faithful Shepherd*, p. 230; Miller, *Colony to Province*, pp. 128 - 129; McLoughlin, *New England Dissent*, I, 49 - 76.

7. *Calendar of State Papers, Colonial Series, America and the West Indies, 1661 - 1668*, pp. 344 - 346.

8. Viola F. Barnes, *The Dominion of New England: A Study in British Colonial Policy* (New Haven, Conn., 1923); Brooks Adams, *The Emancipation of Massachusetts* (Boston, 1962), pp. 349 - 385; Thomas Jefferson Wertenbaker, *The Puritan Oligarchy* (New York, 1947), pp. 316 - 338.

9. Kenneth Murdock, *Increase Mather: The Foremost American Puritan* (Cambridge, Mass., 1925), pp. 211 - 261; Adams, *Emancipation*, p. 375; James Truslow Adams, *The Founding of New England* (Boston, 1921), pp. 426 - 427, 436.

10. Barnes, *Dominion of New England*, pp. 267 - 270.

11. Richard S. Dunn, in *Anglo-American Political Relations, 1675 - 1775*, eds. Alison G. Olson and Richard M. Brown (New Brunswick, N.J., 1970), pp. 72 - 73. Dunn quotes Mather's diary, which is in the Massachusetts Historical Society's collection. The charter of 1691 is published in Francis M. Thorpe, ed., *Federal and State Constitutions, Colonial Charters . . . ,* 7 vols. (Washington, D.C., 1909), III, 1877 - 1883. See also Everett Kimball, *The Public Life of Joseph Dudley* (New York, 1911).

12. Johnson, *A History of New England*, p. 12; Bailyn, *New England Merchants*, pp. 45 - 58.

13. Cotton quoted by Winthrop, in his *History of New England*, ed. Savage, I, 381; *Massachusetts Records*, II, 141; III, 51; Bailyn, *New England Merchants*, pp. 75 - 91, 94 - 106.

14. Higginson, *The Cause of God* (Cambridge, Mass., 1663), p. 12.

15. Ames, *Conscience* (London, 1643), Bk. 5, pp. 248 - 250; Adams, quoted by Miller, *Nature's Nation*, p. 35; Willard, *A Compleat Body of Divinity* (Boston, 1726), p. 695; Moody, *A Practical Discourse* (1685; 2nd ed., Boston, 1746), p. 14; Miller, *Nature's Nation*, p. 48; see also pp. 34 - 49. Weber, *The Protestant Ethic and the Spirit of Capitalism* (London,

1930); Tawney, *Religion and the Rise of Capitalism* (New York, 1926); Little, *Religion, Law, and Order.*

16.   Bailyn, *New England Merchants,* pp. 139, 159 - 160; Rutman, *Winthrop's Boston,* pp. 245 - 250.

17.   Miller, *Colony to Province,* pp. 237 - 247; Bailyn, *New England Merchants,* pp. 37, 135 - 139; Williston Walker, *A History of the Congregational Churches in the United States* (New York, 1894), pp. 199 - 201; Clayton H. Chapman, "The Life and Influence of the Reverend Benjamin Colman," unpublished Ph.D. dissertation, Boston University, 1948, Chapter I.

18.   Chapman, "Colman," Chapter II.

19.   Mather, *Diary,* ed. Ford, I, 326; Miller quotes the verses in *Colony to Province,* p. 244; see also Samuel K. Lothrop, *A History of the Church in Brattle Street* (Boston, 1851); Chapman, "Colman," Chapter II.

20.   Ebenezer Turell quotes Colman in his *The Life and Character of the Reverend Benjamin Colman, D.D.* (Boston, 1749), p. 96; Colman, *The Religious Regards we owe to our Country,* excerpted in *A Library of American Literature,* ed. Edmund C. Stedman and Ellen M. Hutchinson, 11 vols. (New York, 1891), II, 301.

21.   See Thomas A. Shafer, "Solomon Stoddard and the Theology of the Revival," in *A Miscellany of American Christianity,* ed. Stuart C. Henry (Durham, N.C., 1963); Perry Miller, "Solomon Stoddard," *Harvard Theological Review,* 34 (1941), 177 - 320.

22.   Paul R. Lucas, *Valley of Discord: Church and Society along the Connecticut River, 1636 - 1725* (Hanover, N.H., 1976); Miller, *Colony to Province,* p. 471.

23.   Babette May Levy, *Cotton Mather,* forthcoming.

24.   A new edition was begun by Kenneth Murdock. See his Books I and II (Cambridge, Mass., 1975); Murdock, ed., *Selections from Cotton Mather* (New York, 1926); and Bercovitch's essay in *Major Writers,* ed. Emerson.

25.   *Magnalia,* I, 27; Jane Donahue Eberwein, " 'In a book, as in a glas': Literary Sorcery in Mather's Life of Phips," *Early American Literature,* 10 (1975 - 76), 299. See also Bercovitch's essays, in addition to the one previously cited: "New England Epic: Cotton Mather's *Magnalia Christi Americana,*" *ELH,* 33 (1966), 337 - 350, and "Horologicals to Chronometricals," pp. 69 - 74.

26.   Mather, *Magnalia,* I, 27; Miller, *Colony to Province,* pp. 407 - 411; Middlekauf, *The Mathers,* pp. 227 - 230, 305; Mather, *Bonifacius,* ed. Levin, pp. xix - xxi.

27.   Silverman, ed., *Selected Letters of Cotton Mather,* p. 215; Friedrich Heer, *The Intellectual History of Europe* (London, 1966), p. 412.

28.   *Manuductio,* pp. 35 - 37; Kennerly M. Woody, "The 'More Quiet and Hopeful Way,'" *Early American Literature,* 4 (1969 - 70), no. 2, pp. 3 - 48; also the sources Woody cites; Bercovitch essay in *Major Writers,* ed. Emerson, pp. 124 - 126.

29. Silverman, *Selected Letters*, pp. 107 - 110, 337 - 341; Theodore Hornberger in *Early American Literature*, 4 (1969 - 70), no. 1, pp. 43 - 44.

30. Edwards's 1735 "Narrative of Surprising Conversions," in Jonathan Edwards, *Representative Selections*, eds. Clarence Faust and Thomas H. Johnson (New York, 1935), p. 75.

31. Edwin H. Gaustad, *The Great Awakening in New England* (New York, 1957), pp. 16 - 24.

32. Timothy Walker, *The Way to Try all Pretended Apostles* (Boston, 1743), quoted by Gaustad, *Great Awakening*, p. 71; see also Gaustad, pp. 25 - 41.

33. Chauncy, *Seasonable Thoughts*, excerpted in *The Great Awakening*, eds. Alan Heimert and Perry Miller (Indianapolis and New York, 1967), p. 301; Goen, *Revivalism and Separation in New England, 1740 - 1800* (New Haven, Conn., 1962), p. vii.

34. Ahlstrom, *Religious History*, pp. 288, 393 - 394; William W. Sweet, *Religion in Colonial America* (New York, 1951), pp. 311 - 313; Walker, *History of the Congregational Churches*, pp. 27 - 71.

35. See Edward Davison, "From Locke to Edwards," *Journal of the History of Ideas*, 24 (1963), 355 - 372; William J. Scheick, *The Writings of Jonathan Edwards* (College Station, Texas, 1975), p. 141 and passim.

36. See Peter Shaw, *The Character of John Adams* (Chapel Hill, N.C., 1976); Charles H. Foster, *The Rungless Ladder: Harriet Beecher Stowe and New England Puritanism* (Durham, N.C., 1954); Frederic Ives Carpenter, *Emerson Handbook* (New York, 1953), pp. 190 - 203. See also Randall Stewart, "Puritan Literature and the Flowering of New England," *William and Mary Quarterly*, 3rd Series, 3 (1946), 319 - 342. Two recent books worth reading for personal views of the influence of Puritanism in America are Austin Warren, *The New England Conscience* (Ann Arbor, Mich., 1966) and Louis Auchincloss, *The Winthrop Covenant* (New York, 1976).

Selected Bibliography

The notes and references provide a very full guide to the study of Puritanism. The following items are especially recommended.

PRIMARY SOURCES

BRADFORD, William. *Of Plymouth Plantation.* Edited by Samuel Eliot Morison. New York: Alfred A. Knopf, 1952. A modernized text, with notes. Though this edition is the most convenient, it does not supersede the edition of Worthington C. Ford, published in Boston in 1912. Two facsimile editions of the original manuscript are also worth consulting, since Bradford's hand was clear: one was published in London in 1896, the other in Boston, in 1898.

BRADSTREET, ANNE. *The Works of Anne Bradstreet.* Edited by Jeannine Hensley. Cambridge, Mass.: Harvard University Press, 1967. Contains a good essay by Adrienne Rich.

EMERSON, EVERETT, ed. *Letters from New England, 1629 - 1638: The Massachusetts Bay Colony.* Amherst, Mass.: University of Massachusetts Press, 1976. Collects fifty-six letters that tell the story of the creation of the Puritan colony.

HOOKER, THOMAS. *Redemption: Three Sermons.* Gainesville, Fla.: Scholars' Facsimiles and Reprints, 1956. A convenient facsimile edition.

LECHFORD, THOMAS. *Plain Dealing: or, Newes from New England.* London, 1642. An unsympathetic look at the Puritans by a one-time resident of Massachusetts. A good edition is that of J. Hammond Trumbull, published in Boston in 1867. It has been re-issued.

MATHER, COTTON. *Selections.* Edited by Kenneth B. Murdock. New York: Harcourt, Brace, 1926; reissued, New York: Hafner, 1960. A good sampling of *Magnalia Christi Americana* and parts of *The Christian Philosopher.* A new edition of the *Magnalia*, edited by Murdock, has begun to appear.

MESEROLE, HARRISON T., ed. *Seventeenth-Century American Poetry.* Garden City, New York: Doubleday, 1968. An excellent anthology, with many Puritan poets represented.

MILLER, PERRY, and THOMAS H. JOHNSON, eds. *The Puritans: A Sourcebook of Their Writings.* New York: Harper and Row, 1963. A learned edition, with very good prefatory essays.

PLUMSTEAD, A. W., ed. *The Wall and the Garden: Selected Massachusetts Election Sermons, 1670 - 1775.* Minneapolis: University of Minnesota Press, 1968. Contains many jeremiads.

173

TAYLOR, EDWARD. *The Poems of Edward Taylor*. Edited by Donald E. Stanford. New Haven, Conn.: Yale University Press, 1960. A very well-prepared collection of Taylor's best verse.

VAUGHAN, ALDEN T., ed. *The Puritan Tradition in America, 1620 - 1730*. New York: Harper and Row, 1972. More historically oriented than Miller and Johnson's collection.

SECONDARY SOURCES

BERCOVITCH, SACVAN, ed. *Typology and Early American Literature*. Amherst, Mass.: University of Massachusetts Press, 1972. Treats fully an aspect of Puritanism largely neglected by even such penetrating scholars as Miller and Morgan.

COOLIDGE, JOHN S. *The Pauline Renaissance in England: Puritanism and the Bible*. Oxford: Clarendon, 1970. A neglected study that offers the best explanation of the split between Puritanism and Anglicanism in England.

ELLIOTT, EMORY. *Power and the Pulpit in Puritan New England*. Princeton: Princeton University Press, 1975. The first study by a student of literature to take advantage of the important studies of Massachusetts towns by Powell, Rutman, Lockridge, and Greven. Focuses on the second generation.

HALL, DAVID D. *The Faithful Shepherd: A History of the New England Ministry in the Seventeenth Century*. Chapel Hill: University of North Carolina Press, 1972. An authoritative study that deals with nearly every aspect of American Puritanism and examines the evolving nature of the phenomenon.

HALLER, WILLIAM. *The Rise of Puritanism*. New York: Columbia University Press, 1938. A warm, humanistic study of early seventeenth-century English Puritanism.

JENNINGS, FRANCIS. *The Invasion of America: Indians, Colonialism, and the Cant of Conquest*. Chapel Hill: University of North Carolina Press, 1975. A revisionist history of Puritan-Indian relationships. Persuasive.

KELLER, KARL. *The Example of Edward Taylor*. Amherst, Mass.: University of Massachusetts Press, 1975. A witty general study.

MCGIFFERT, MICHAEL. "American Puritan Studies in the 1960s," *William & Mary Quarterly*, 3rd ser., 28 (1970), 36 - 67. A careful examination of the work of Perry Miller and later students of the topic that he brought so to the attention of scholars.

MIDDLEKAUF, ROBERT. *The Mathers: Three Generations of Puritan Intellectuals, 1596 - 1728*. New York: Oxford University Press, 1971. Offers an extended corrective to the work of Perry Miller, and a general interpretation, as well, of the whole phenomenon of Puritanism.

MILLER, PERRY. *Orthodoxy in Massachusetts, 1630 - 1650.* Cambridge, Mass.: Harvard University Press, 1933. Miller's dissertation, a study of the origins of Massachusetts Bay Congregationalism. Best read in the 1970 edition, with preface by David Hall.

———. *The New England Mind: The Seventeenth Century.* Cambridge, Mass.: Harvard University Press, 1939. A very demanding, highly intellectual study of American Puritanism. Though now frequently challenged and corrected, a fundamental study.

———. *The New England Mind: From Colony to Province.* Cambridge, Mass.: Harvard University Press, 1953. More readable than the previous title, this book examines the evolution of Puritanism from 1650 till about 1725.

———. *Errand into the Wilderness.* Cambridge, Mass.: Harvard University Press, 1956. An important collection of Miller's essays, others of which appear in his posthumous *Nature's Nation.* Cambridge, Mass., 1967.

MORGAN, EDMUND S. *The Puritan Family: Religion and Domestic Relations in Seventeenth Century New England.* Boston: Trustees of the Public Library, 1944; revised and enlarged, New York: Harper and Row, 1966. A pleasant book to dip into. Morgan's Harvard dissertation.

———. *The Puritan Dilemma: The Story of John Winthrop.* Boston: Little, Brown, 1958. Combines biography of the leader of the Massachusetts Bay colony with a brilliant interpretation and appreciation of the colony's rationale.

———. *Roger Williams: The Church and the State.* New York: Harcourt Brace, 1967. Another lucid volume, the most interesting and most important on Roger Williams, with valuable sidelights on Massachusetts Bay Puritanism.

———. *Visible Saints: The History of a Puritan Idea.* New York: New York University Press, 1963. A marvellously clear and groundbreaking study of the Congregational ideal of the church of the elect.

MURDOCK, KENNETH B. *Increase Mather: The Foremost American Puritan.* Cambridge, Mass.: Harvard University Press, 1925. A long and somewhat labored dissertation but still worth reading for its treatment of a central figure. An easier way to meet Increase Mather is through Mason I. Lowance, Jr., *Increase Mather.* New York: Twayne, 1974.

———. *Literature & Theology in Colonial New England.* Cambridge, Mass.: Harvard University Press, 1949. More specifically literary than most of the previous volumes.

RUTMAN, DARRETT B. *Winthrop's Boston: A Portrait of a Puritan Town, 1630 - 1649.* Chapel Hill: University of North Carolina Press, 1965. A readable study of the Puritan center.

STANFORD, ANN. *Anne Bradstreet: The Worldly Puritan.* New York: Burt
     Franklin, 1974. An attractive study of the poet and her poems.
ZIFF, LARZER. *Puritanism in America: New Culture in a New World.* New
     York: Viking, 1973. A sophisticated recent study.

Index